AF588139

SANJAY DUTT

SANJAY DUTT

One Man, Many Lives

Ram Kamal Mukherjee

RUPA

Published by
Rupa Publications India Pvt. Ltd 2019
7/16, Ansari Road, Daryaganj
New Delhi 110002

Sales centres:
Allahabad Bengaluru Chennai
Hyderabad Jaipur Kathmandu
Kolkata Mumbai

ISBN: 978-93-5333-452-9

First impression 2019

10 9 8 7 6 5 4 3 2 1

Printed by Parksons Graphics Pvt. Ltd., Mumbai

To Nari Hira,
the man who taught me to be fearless and honest.

To Ma, Baba and Sarbani,
for being my pillars of strength, always.

Contents

Author's Note

Why another book on Sanjay Dutt?

Do I know him? Does he inspire me? Is he the best actor in Indian cinema? I would not respond in the affirmative to any of these questions.

Then, why write about Sanjay Dutt?

More than his status as an actor or a celebrity, it is the human side of Sanjay Dutt that appealed to me the most. He was the back-bencher in class who had the most fascinating stories to tell. He was the man who wanted to set things right every time he failed. He was the prodigal son who was ostracized by people in the film fraternity, while his popularity among his fans remained undiminished. His enigma remained unshaken.

In the past two years of my research on Sanju Baba, one thing became apparent—he is by far the most misunderstood man in Indian cinema. In the process of penning my narrative I discovered a star-kid who messed up, but, with the passage of time, eventually managed to set things right.

Along the way came Rajkumar Hirani's biopic *Sanju*. I expected to see the real Dutt, finally. Unfortunately, the film was more fiction than fact. Only one aspect of the film stayed with me—the unspoken yet riveting bond between Sunil Dutt and Sanjay. Ever since the film, my respect for Dutt sahab went up. And, perhaps, I felt bad for man-child Sanju.

Immediately after the film, Sanjay Dutt announced that he was writing his own memoirs. That's when I decided to revisit my approach to this book and write this not as a biography, but as a case study. This book will tell you the story of a Bollywood superstar who went through fire and came out alive.

To make this book authentic and factually correct, I have refrained from hearsay anecdotes and the many stories on Dutt that keep 'floating'.

I hope you will enjoy reading the book, which is nothing less than a 70-mm blockbuster release.

Prologue

A few months before Rajkumar Hirani was to release his Sanjay Dutt biopic, *Sanju,* Yasser Usman's 'unauthorized biography' of the actor was hurriedly released to make the most of the fresh surge in curiosity around the controversial star. The *Crazy Untold Story of Bollywood's Bad Boy* took a meticulous look at Dutt's colourful life, his brushes with the law and the underworld, his addiction and his unravelling. Dutt responded by slamming the book and threatening to drag the publishers to court. He vowed to tell his story in his own words, when the time was right. He dismissed the book, alleging that it was based only on gossip magazines, and blamed the media for perpetuating what he said were 'figments of imagination.'

And then *Sanju* released. For weeks, hundreds and thousands of cinegoers took up every seat in every theatre to watch an elaborate work of fiction being paraded as fact. Rajkumar Hirani had not failed his friend. Or his friend's wife—who had requested Hirani to make a film on her 'ill-fated', 'wronged' husband, who she believed was trapped in a media trial. *Sanju* was the mother of all PR spiels. Dutt would never again need an interview, article or chat session to convince the world that he was never the bad boy we believed him to be. The film was Hirani's most dishonest piece of work. Always with a finger on the pulse of his audience and never one for subtlety, Hirani painted *Sanju* with all the broad strokes and heavy handedness of a daily vernacular soap. And the scheming, villainous mother-in-law's role was played by the 'media.'

But the audiences were as generous and forgiving to Sanjay Dutt's screen avatar—to his carefully crafted story—as they had been to the man before. As they were to Hirani's narrative, in which Dutt's many affairs and abusive relationships, his trysts with the underworld and politics and his run-ins with the law were either ignored or simplified beyond recognition. What remained was his long battle with drugs and his periodic efforts to salvage himself and rise in the estimation of his father.

Most importantly—after having blamed his father and sisters all his life for his unravelling, in the film he pinned the blame on the media. Of all the labels that had stuck to him, Dutt was particularly concerned with the tag of 'terrorist'. In his mind, he had paid the price for being a rogue of a son, a heartbreaker and a bad father to his firstborn. He spoke candidly about all his issues. But he could not handle being tried for illegal possession of arms and for his links to the terrorists accused in the 1993 Mumbai bombings. It bothered him. Crushed his father. Ravaged his family. From incredulity—*I am Sanjay Dutt, how could this happen to me?*—to denial to surrender and finally to defiance, he traversed a whole character arc. But not so much in the film as in real life.

So who is Sanjay Dutt? The first star-kid to be in the limelight for all the wrong reasons? A man who has been to hell and back—and loves telling the tale? A man with the intelligence of an adolescent and no sense of consequence? A star-kid with a disturbing sense of entitlement, grounded only by reality? Or simply a myth, created and perpetuated by the star himself and the complicit film media of the '90s?

Perhaps he is all of that and more.

The Sanjay Dutt saga is far from over. There is still another book in the works, allegedly written by the star himself—where, no doubt, he will present his version of every incident that shaped his life. By then, we will perhaps have a *Rashomon*-esque view of his life. It is worth revisiting the story of Sanjay Dutt as often as possible, for it is likely to throw up more subtexts, surprises and insights with every reading. Likewise, it is important to read the Dutt story with a critical eye—strip it of its glamour and the romance of the dark and the tragic.

It is a life that sums up Bollywood in all its patriarchy, sexism, nepotism and clique culture. The bro codes, the misogyny, the dark side of stardom. And as long as we pay to watch his films, there will always be interest in how a star rose, fell, and got back on his shiny feet again.

It is tough to peel off the layers and get to the real story of Sanjay Dutt. To look past his attempts to whitewash his crimes or give them a sympathetic spin. Because Sanjay Dutt is not just the son of India's two most venerated matinee idols. He is a product of the myth-making machine that is Bollywood. Right from the day the very first article about him appeared, through many a gossip piece and scathing interview of the star and his friends and foes, under the relentless gaze of the crime reporters who dissected his role in the bombings, the myth of Sanjay Dutt has been in the telling. And even as he spends his quieter years as a free man, it still is.

1

A Bundle of Hope

On 29 July 1959, at precisely 2.45 p.m., two of the country's biggest stars—Nargis and Sunil Dutt—were blessed with a gorgeous baby boy. The baby had dreamy eyes that would eventually make hundreds of women swoon. His little arms would someday grow to Grecian perfection. And his tiny mouth would eventually curl into a deadly half-smile, dangling a lit cigarette with the rakish charm of a devil that never cared.

But all that would be in the distant future—many eventful and tumultuous years later.

On this day, however, the beautiful mother and the handsome father cradled their bundle of hope—a symbol of their unconventional love story and rare inter-faith marriage. Just a decade after Independence, with the scars of the partition still raw and the country poised for giant leaps into the global arena, they were hopeful for a different future for their firstborn. They believed that their Sanjay—their Sanju Baba—was destined for greatness. After all, the apple never really falls far from the tree, does it?

Decades later—in the midst of a raging controversy that would destroy his life—Sunil Dutt would recall this day in an emotional conversation with television host Farooq Sheikh. 'Sanju had arrived at a very important time in our lives,' Dutt sahab (as he was called by the masses that loved him) would say. 'Both Nargis and I had been through a lot. And he brought us unbridled joy.'

It is said that those born on this date are imaginative and artsy. But they are also unable to escape their destiny and the tragic flaws in their characters. They are unable to handle stressful situations, prone to emotional breakdowns and constantly in need of validation for their love. As children, they feel like outcasts even in the most loving environments. And even in their mature years, they are unable to outgrow the child within.

★

Born in Calcutta (now Kolkata), Nargis, known as Baby Rani in the early years of her life, was the daughter of Jaddanbai, a star of the talkies in those days.

Jaddanbai was the darling of Calcutta's social circuit at that time. Aristocrats from the city spent hours at her apartment with their European guests, enjoying her music and company. The soirees were sparkling and decadent. But soon an economic crisis hit the vibrant city, the brown sahibs disappeared and the charmed bubble burst, forcing Jaddan to leave for Bombay (now Mumbai), the city of promises. She moved to Chateau Marine—on Marine Drive in Bombay—which also drew the likes of film producer Kamal Amrohi and actor Dilip Kumar, with their own colourful soirees and mehfils. Nargis grew up in a world of male adulation and coquetry and her childhood was sacrificed at the altar of fame and fortune.

Sunil Dutt, on the other hand, had a far less glamorous beginning. Born Balraj Dutt, he belonged to a family that lost pretty much everything during the partition. In 1950, twenty-year-old Balraj arrived in Bombay, penniless, luckless and running low on hope. But life and the city of endless possibilities were willing to give him a chance. Balraj somehow landed the lead role in *Railway Platform*, a film that changed his—and his family's—fortunes for good.

The two actors, Nargis and Sunil, born under two very different sets of circumstances and families, were thrown together in one of the most iconic films ever made—*Mother India*.

On 1 March 1957, Nargis and Sunil Dutt were enacting the now-famous scene involving a village fire. The complex scene had Radha (Nargis) in a field of burning haystacks, frantically looking for her bandit son, Birju (Sunil Dutt). The two earnest actors had insisted on shooting without body doubles. Suddenly, the wind changed directions and the raging flames engulfed Nargis. Dutt grabbed a blanket and plunged into the circle of fire, rescuing the woman who would be his wife.

For the next few days, the two actors, who had both sustained burns, were drawn close to each other. Nargis, who had been nursing a broken heart since her painful relationship with Raj Kapoor, was deeply touched by Dutt's simplicity and unconditional affection. Even though she wanted to get married before the film released, the couple was advised against it—the audience would never have accepted a real-life couple as screen mother and child. They married a year later, in a simple ceremony—setting the bar for an industry that would not see such a strong, devoted couple again in many years.

*

Sunil Dutt's traumatic experience during the partition had left indelible scars on his soul and shaped his personality—especially as a father.

The hardships he had had to go through after losing everything that his father had earned made him take a rather severe view towards parenting. While Nargis, who was naturally gifted, was far more generous with her love, wisdom and patience, Dutt was her antithesis. His love for his family and his commitment towards their well-being was unquestionable, but Dutt remained guarded in his expressions of affection. He was never a man to wear his heart on his sleeves. Like so many parents of that time, he believed that hardships and the strictest discipline built character.

While Nargis and Sunil Dutt would ideally have played the good cop–bad cop routine that most Indian parents are wont to do in their lifetimes, the sharp difference in their world views and approach to parenting seeded the conflict that defined their firstborn. Dutt may have been far more indulgent with his daughters—Namrata and Priya—but with Sanjay, he was exceptionally harsh. 'We were also extremely indulgent,' he confessed to Farooq Sheikh in the same interview, 'because he brought us so much happiness.' Dutt seldom expressed his love during his son's formative years, yet circumstances and destiny saw him take every blow for his son's gravest errors and misdemeanours as long as he was alive. Never lacking in respect and love because of his incredible moral rectitude and his compassion for the underdog, Dutt sahab's stature was only enhanced once his son's misdeeds began to go public. And that was the irony. Despite being hauled over the coals of humiliation because of his son, he had the image of a battle-scarred, lonely warrior, who stood by the very same son. Because he knew that's exactly what his beloved wife would have wanted. His fans, his followers and those whose lives he had transformed as a social worker and a member of parliament (MP), only had the deepest sympathy for him. They saw him as a man whose life was all about stumbling from one tragedy to another. A man who deserved much more for his legendary dedication to his wife, his country and his family. He was a hero.

A textbook tragic hero.

Noted film writer Bhawana Somaaya shone some light into the heart of darkness that was the Dutt home, in an article for *The Quint*:

> In 1991 I did an exhaustive interview with Sunil Dutt, in which he described his life as a 'house of heartbreaks'. Dutt shared pages from his past and said that he had repressed memories for so long that it was a catharsis to be speaking to me. He showed the supplementary booklet carrying my interview on all his friends and shared that now he was

inspired to write an autobiography. He never did so, but he systematically documented memories in a special drawer and after he was gone, his daughters were so moved by the rare pictures/personal letters/notes on his characters and roles, that they took a collective decision to compile these memories into a book called *Mr and Mrs Dutt: Memories of Our Parents*.'

*

Sanjay Dutt's story is unique. While the Kapoors, from Raj to Rishi and more, were already there and their personal lives made for rich gossip fodder, their dalliances were nothing in comparison to this rockstar of a son that Sunil and Nargis Dutt had produced.

If, on the one hand, he was born privileged, on the other, he was suffering for the same. The mother went overboard with her affections; the father never cut him any slack. Add to this the fact that the world that Sanjay found himself in—the film industry of the time, especially the posh neighbourhood of Bandra—was teeming with choices, mostly of the dubious kind. Sanjay, born in a new, affluent India, was insulated from the horrors of the partition. Nor was he aware of or affected by the humiliation his mother had had to face for being a child actress born to an entertainer. He grew up wrapped in cotton wool, in the midst of affluent, influential friends, and it was easy for him to take everything for granted. Everything that both his parents, in their own ways, had to fight for. Acceptance. Validation. Money.

In fact, many years later, in an interview to a TV channel, Sanjay Dutt made light of his foray into films by saying that he became an actor because he had nothing else to do.

This statement, made in jest, was probably far from the truth. Sunil and Nargis Dutt were hugely respected stars in their time. Dutt, as mentioned before, was known for his moral rectitude. He could be obstinate about his values and beliefs, but his decision to get his son into the film industry was not a casual one. He was aware of his legacy; his son was not. Perhaps it would dawn upon the son later that for every door that opened for him thanks to his famous last name, there awaited a grievous pitfall. He was never rated highly as an actor. And despite carrying his mother's genes, he struggled to emote. What he did have—something he was born with—was swag: that intangible, iridescent glow of stardom that only a handful can claim to possess. In the Hindi film industry, where the first appearance of a male lead is usually heralded with drum rolls and trumpet calls, Dutt was cut out for the job.

Why, then, did Dutt's life turn out the way it did? A critical view would call it hubris. A sympathetic one would say it was just bad choices and bad luck. A fatalist would wonder why every time he seemed to be getting back on track, something would go horribly wrong. The fan would chuckle at how, despite all his fallings and series of errors in judgments, his audiences kept going back to watch his films. And his detractors would throw up their hands and wonder how it is that someone with such limited talent has always found an opportunity to prove himself, over and over again.

When logic fails and empirical evidence is unable to drive an argument, it is best to leave everything to accident. Fate. Because stars are more than the sum total of their blood, sweat, tears, laughter and affairs. There is also that X-factor, that invisible presence that calls the shots in their lives and pulls the strings from beyond our field of vision. Their stories are the coming together of the real, the fantastic, the tragic and the darkly comic. They seem to follow no scripts, but have all the makings of a potboiler.

This story is an attempt to understand the 'script', such as it is, of the first-ever rockstar of Hindi cinema.

2

A Courtroom Drama

16 May 2013

A scene from a Hindi potboiler or one from a slice-of-life drama? It was a bit of both as Sanjay Dutt's vehicle drove into the narrow lane of the City Civil and Sessions Court in South Mumbai around 2.30 p.m. He was immediately surrounded by fans, reporters and camerapersons. The crowd swelled, chanting slogans in his support. Others almost wailed as scenes of emotional outpouring greeted the star. There was a tussle between his fans and camerapersons who were trying to get as close to him as possible.

His friend, filmmaker Mahesh Bhatt, came out of the car first with arms folded, requesting the media to give Dutt some space so that he could reach the court. Inside the court, Dutt, dressed in a crisp white kurta and blue jeans, was led by his lawyer Rizwan Merchant—who claimed the actor had been roughed up by several persons. Dutt was wearing a red tilak and religious threads around his neck. His face was pallid. As the court began the proceedings, he held on to his wife's hand and the two whispered consolations to each other.

Dutt was to complete the remaining forty-two months of his sentences for the 1993 Mumbai serial bombing case.

His lawyer presented a list of 'basic amenities' for Dutt—a thin mattress, a fan, medicines for arterial stenosis and high cholesterol, and permission to move around the jail. After all, he argued, his client was not asking for any luxury items. He said that Dutt was a chain smoker and sought permission for him to be allowed to use medicinal electronic cigarettes. The court instead asked Dutt to quit smoking.

*

25 February 2017

It was a bright morning. At precisely 8 a.m. the massive gates of Yerwada Jail opened, and out stepped Sanjay Dutt wearing a dark blue shirt and jeans.

At 8.15 a.m., he turned around near the gate to face the prison and bowed. He saluted the Indian tri-colour fluttering on top of the prison wall.

A little further away, Rajkumar Hirani, the man who gave Dutt the lifeline called *Munna Bhai,* was filming this moment. It would eventually make its way into the biopic that he had been making.

At 8.20 a.m., Dutt greeted his family and friends outside the jail. Besides Hirani, there were his wife Manyata, writer Abhijat Joshi, Dutt's lawyers, hundreds of fans and the media. Dutt paused, addressed the media and credited his fans for their unflinching support. And his words—telecast live by Times Now and scores of other channels—were heavy with dark humour, the weight of experience and the smell of fatalism. He smiled—a shadow of his famous half-curl—and said, '*Mujhe Raju ne signing amount nahin dia hai yeh shoot karne ke liye* (Rajkumar Hirani has not paid me a signing amount for shooting this scene).' It was evident that his equation with Hirani had in fact grown strong over time and controversies. But the real picture would emerge only a year later, when *Sanju* the biopic released.

Before heading for the iconic Siddhivinayak Temple in Mumbai, Dutt turned to the camerapersons once more and thanked his fans: 'I am here because of their support and there is no easy road to freedom, my friends.'

There was a similar scene at the popular temple in the south of Mumbai. Members of the media had been waiting for over four hours to capture the moment. Sporting a tonsured look with a chhoti (short ponytail), Dutt walked inside the temple, past the sea of humanity, holding Manyata's hand as firmly as he could. He handed over ₹840—his earnings from the five years in jail—to Manyata. She let the tears flow. It was perhaps the most precious gift she had ever received from her husband.

Dutt proceeded to perform the Ganesh aarti and took blessings from the priest—almost as if he wanted to go through a cleansing process.

In the evening, he addressed the media again, outside his Bandra residence. He confessed that he was still coming to terms with the fact that he was finally out of jail and spending time with his wife, sisters and kids. 'It took twenty-three years for me to be a free man. Finally I am a free man. But it is taking time for the fact that I am a free man to sink in. The person that I am missing the most is my father. If he had been alive, he would have been the happiest person. His only battle in life was to set his son free,' Dutt paused. He looked up tearfully at the sky and continued, 'Dad, I am free today!' As with everything else in his life, this intensely personal experience was broadcast on news channels.

Dutt added that he spoke to his mother at her grave: 'I went to her grave and told her, "*Ma aaj main azaad ho gaya* (Mom, I am free now)." I am sure even she was worried about me.' He paused and gulped. Manyata, standing right behind, pressed his shoulder reassuringly.

If Dutt was celebrating the end of a nightmare that had lasted for twenty-three years, his wife—often referred to as his 'best half', not simply 'better'—had fought her own battles in the interim. She seemed to have come out stronger and was now there for him like a rock, as always.

But the ordeal was not exactly over. A lot had changed between the time Dutt first went to prison for the illegal arms possession case and the time he finally finished his prison term at Yerwada.

The media—and social media—was especially unforgiving about his repeated paroles. Mere hours after he walked a free man, he was questioned again on whether his celebrity status had won him the paroles. 'I disagree with that,' Dutt replied firmly. 'The *aam aadmi* gets many more facilities... Due to constant scrutiny and my celebrity status, I had to go through far stricter rules.'

The four days leading up to his freedom were perhaps the longest, for the man who had been in and out of jail more than any public figure in post-Independence India. 'The concept of freedom was seeping into my soul. I wanted to come out clean, once and for all—for my parents, my wife and kids. I didn't want to be called a terrorist, and when the honorable Supreme Court judge declared that I am not a terrorist, that was my victory. I wanted my dad to witness that moment. He had wanted to hear those words from the court of law.'

What struck an emotional note was Dutt's deference for Manyata, wondering at how she managed to keep the show going with their toddlers and handle his finances in his absence. '*Mujhe toh jail mein daal roti mil jaati thi, par inki chinta mujhe jail mein khaai jaati thi* (I would get roti and dal to eat in the jail, but worry for my family would eat me up),' he added. Manyata's face was almost a mask. Her eyes, the only things that could have betrayed her turmoil, were hidden behind enormous sunglasses. There was no camera in the world that could capture her vulnerability.

Dutt pleaded with the media once again, 'The Supreme Court booked me under the Arms Act, and I have served the punishment for the same. The charges against me regarding the '93 bombings, brought under TADA, have been dismissed. I am not a terrorist, so please don't refer to me as one.'

Just like any edgy thriller, this could have been the last scene of his biopic. Or maybe not. Sanjay Dutt was probably—finally—coming to terms with the fact that when it comes to destiny, you can run but you cannot hide.

*

Early fame and adulation, a long bout of drug addiction and the fight to overcome it, a string of relationships that he was accused of destroying and a tumultuous relationship with his own family—none of these could change the love and adulation that Dutt's fans had for him. Because nothing captures the imagination of the Indian audiences and brings out their inner Gandhi better than a repentant man. And Dutt—who was never really a skilled actor on screen—played this off-screen role to the hilt.

There are very few stars who would confess to their own inadequacies, frailties and mistakes. The bluntness with which Dutt repeatedly admitted to his mistakes—the candour and artlessness with which he detailed his drug addiction—were different from the way he hid his connections with the underworld. But the world would come to know of this much, much later. For the most part of his life, he won over even his staunchest critics with his 'honesty' and his seemingly profound philosophy: 'There is no drug in the world that I haven't done… For me, life has not been beautiful. It has been like climbing Mount Everest and then falling. But every time I climbed, I reached the top—*beech mein nahin gira* (I didn't fall in the middle).'

Over and over again, in his many interviews to every willing media person who was charmed by his bad-boy-with-a-golden-heart narrative, he blamed his father, his mother's death, his friends and later the underworld and the media for every misstep, every crime and every woman he cheated on. Perhaps he did suffer all the injustices and tragedies. But in his relentless quest for sympathy and success, he was also guilty of manipulating public opinion. And the media—till it tired of him.

The story of Sanjay Dutt is not so much about a star-son's public tryst with the law but of a man's never-ending battle with the demons of his mind—and the consequences of his reckless choices.

3

The Scars of Lawrence

Despite his public image of a little boy trapped in a man's body, Sanjay Dutt was far from a simple guy to know. There is sufficient evidence in the public domain to prove that the seeds of his complex personality were sown during his impressionable years, when communication between him and his father nearly broke down. The forceful separation from his mother, who he was very attached to, would leave indelible scars.

By all accounts, he has had a very unusual life.

Being the only son of star parents, one would expect Sanjay to be pampered, since he was born with the proverbial golden spoon in his mouth. But he turned out to be a rebellious youngster whose tryst with drugs began at a very early age.

In a book she wrote about her parents, *Mr and Mrs Dutt,* Namrata Dutt spoke of the near-idyllic childhood of the Dutt siblings. Vacations were family affairs—just the parents and the three siblings, Sanjay, Priya and Namrata, in Europe.

Nargis was a fun-loving person and a great swimmer, recalls Namrata. As a young girl, she used to play cricket and football with her brothers. She was the quintessential tomboy. Nargis was never really the kind of person who wore the halo of stardom around her. She would happily eat pani puri from the chaatwala down the road and watch movies in a theatre. She didn't wear a burkha and loved having long conversations on the telephone. And she was happy to give up stardom, preferring the life of a homemaker. She would supervise the cooking and would sometimes cook herself. She would pick up recipes and perfect them.

In Namrata's view, they had a perfect home—but something was not quite right. Namrata and Sanjay were two-and-a-half years apart and were good friends; they rarely fought and enjoyed the same music. Priya Dutt was five years junior to them. But Sanjay, says Namrata, was a born rebel. Even as a kid, he would pick up his father's cigarette stubs to take puffs. In an interview with *Stardust* in 2001, Sanjay Dutt admitted that he was caught by his father the first time he smoked. 'I was barely nine years old or so. I managed to take a leftover from the ash tray and was smoking on the terrace, when my father spotted me. He did what a father should do and I quickly ran behind my mother—literally behind her pallu—seeking help. She saved me that day, but I knew that if I got caught again, then it would be my last day in this house.' Sometimes even Nargis would get angry with Sanjay and would verbally abuse him or beat him up.

This coincided with a particularly tough phase in Sunil Dutt's life. Very few people know that Sanjay Dutt started out as a child actor in his father's film *Reshma Aur Shera* at the age of twelve, playing a qawwali singer. Though the film fetched Sunil global accolades from the Berlin Film Festival and even got selected as India's official entry at the 44th Academy Awards, the box-office collections were not promising enough to save Sunil's sinking career as an actor. The failure of *Reshma Aur Shera* in 1971 had almost wiped out Dutt's savings and his currency in the industry as an actor and filmmaker. He was in debt of ₹35 lakh, a staggering amount in those days. For the first time in Dutt sahab's life, ruthless creditors were hounding him, humiliating him. It wasn't really a happy situation. To keep Sanjay away from unsettling influences—and to save him from himself—he was packed off to The Lawrence School in Sanawar.

The school, founded by Sir Henry Lawrence and his wife Honoria, is one of the oldest surviving boarding schools. The family hoped that in the natural surroundings of the residential school, Dutt would become more grounded. But the rebellious and sensitive child began to feel that he had been abandoned by his busy parents. In recent years, during a chat session with noted journalist Soma Choudhary at Algebra in New Delhi, Sanjay Dutt admitted, 'It was actually Mrs Gandhi (Prime Minister Indira Gandhi) who suggested to my mom that she should send me off to a boarding school—that it would keep me away from "bad" influence. But then, she (Nargis) did not know that in the very backyard of our school was a mountain where marijuana was cultivated.' Mr and Mrs Dutt were committed Congress party workers and there was no way they could have ignored the party supremo's well-meaning advice.

Sanjay Dutt was ragged and bullied, says Namrata in *Mr and Mrs Dutt*. He would write long, anguished letters to his mother, saying 'I miss you, I love you, I want to come home.' She would write back to console him and often drive off to him at Sanawar. But he longed to be back at home—though Sunil Dutt was of the opinion that Sanjay needed to be disciplined.

Sanjay Dutt confessed to Choudhury in the chat, 'My friends—I call them friends now—would call me tractor, because I was the son of an actor. And they would consider me a dumb kid from Mumbai, who had no ambition in life. I would terribly miss home, especially my mom.'

This elite institution is the alma mater for several high-profile people. Naturally, no one was expected to treat the only son of Nargis and Sunil Dutt as just another schoolmate. Sanjay was taller than most of his classmates and exceptionally good-looking—things that made him popular. His group was known for their brand of mischief and indulged in pranks. While he had had his share of being bullied, tormented and subjected to exceptional disciplinarian actions, he was eventually the boy everyone wanted to be friends with.

But the teachers at Lawrence treated him with a kind of hostility. Far from being treated with kid gloves, Dutt was subjected to unprecedented harshness because of his celebrity background. 'It was like ten of us would do something and he would be the one who got punished until he dislocated a shoulder', a friend said in an interview later. 'School teachers everywhere can be sadistic but they really had it in for Sanju, as if they had a point to prove,' writes Suketu Mehta in his book. A particularly standout passage describes how Dutt was made to crawl up a gravel slope until his hands and knees bled. The next day, the bandages were torn off and he was made to repeat the exercise. And all this was so different from the world he had in Bombay, where he was a star child surrounded by parents, cousins, aunts and helpers, adored and indulged. Sanju kept most people at a distance, but he did make some very close friends in school and is still in touch with them.

At middle school, Sanjay not only made peace with the rough and tumble, disciplinarian, almost sadistic treatment meted out to him, he actually fell in love with his independence at the boarding. When he came home after school and joined Elphinstone College, he was not interested in academics and got into the kind of company that would prove to be his undoing.

By the time Dutt finished school, he had started feeling resentful—an emotion that had been alien to him till then. On a TV show with Simi Garewal in 2007, he said that when parents send their kid away to a boarding school, the kid has to learn to be independent. 'When I came home to find that they wanted to tell me what to do, it irritated me. And that is why I started hanging out with friends who took recreational drugs—what began with a little bit of weed turned into nine years of hell.'

Once he returned to Bombay, there was a certain void in his life, which he tried to fill with video games, arguments, violent fights—and by threatening neighbours with an air gun. And no matter how hard his sisters tried, they could not keep him out of trouble. It was around this time that the news of Nargis being detected with cancer was shared with the family. Young Dutt made a valiant attempt to control and hide his emotions, but he was a complete wreck. Despite being so close to his mother, when Nargis finally passed away, Sanjay was so high on drugs that he was not even aware of the loss that he had just suffered.

Nargis often wondered why Sanjay would keep himself locked up in his room. It was only a matter of time before she realized that he was smoking marijuana. Unfortunately, at that time, Nargis's health had begun to deteriorate and no matter how hard she tried or how much she wanted, she couldn't really monitor her son. Sunil Dutt, likewise, had no time for Sanjay because he was busy taking care of his wife.

Namrata was in her second year of college when Nargis fell seriously ill for the first time. It began with a variant of jaundice and then quickly developed into pancreatic cancer. She was moved to the Sloan and Kettering Cancer Center in New York in 1980. There she underwent a complicated surgery to remove the pancreas. Though the procedure seemed to be successful at first, Nargis started haemorrhaging within twenty-four hours and slipped into a coma for four months. These were the most trying months for the Dutt family. Namrata, Priya and Sunil Dutt stayed with Nargis in the US where Dutt sahab had taken on the role of mother, nurse, friend and caregiver. He would feed his wife, clean her and brush her teeth. The family lived in an apartment close to the hospital. He never shared his feelings with his children, but the daughters recall that he would often cry silently in his room. They had run out of funds and the struggling stalwart began to borrow money for her treatment.

Four months later, when Nargis finally got back on her feet, people began to call her 'The Miracle Lady'. Namrata writes: 'The first day she took a few steps with the help of a walker, everyone clapped.' Nargis eventually came home in April 1981. Their house in Bandra had turned into a makeshift hospital. But despite the air of optimism and the fervent prayers, Nargis slipped into a coma once again and passed away on 3 May 1981. She was only fifty-two years old.

Nargis was not present at the premiere of *Rocky*, Sanjay Dutt's debut on 7 May, just four days after her demise. As a touching tribute, her seat was kept vacant next to Sunil Dutt. In an interview with British Broadcasting Corporation (BBC) in 1996 for a documentary film on Sanjay Dutt, Sunil Dutt said, 'Just three days before the premiere of *Rocky*, she passed away. We didn't know what had hit us. For us, the premiere show of your debut film is probably the biggest and happiest day of one's career. I didn't know whether to celebrate or mourn.'

Sanjay recalled that day in an interview with *Stardust* in 2003: 'I still remember that my dad kept a seat empty beside him at the premiere show. Some gentleman walked up to him and requested if he could be seated in that chair, to that my dad replied, "No, that's for my wife!"'

*

Sunil Dutt's whole life revolved around Nargis. After her death, he simply fell apart. It further embittered his already fragile relationship with Sanjay. However, one day the actor-filmmaker simply snapped out of his depression and decided that it was time to get back to work. Namrata went back to college, Priya went back to school. Everyone wanted to reclaim their lives. Everyone, except the son.

In the BBC interview, Sanjay admitted that he was so stoned during his mother's last few days that he didn't even realize that she had passed away. 'It actually took me two years to realize that I had lost my mother forever. That's when I realized what harm drugs did to me. I had no emotions left in me. I wanted to mourn my mother's death, I wanted to tell her that I loved her the most, but I was too dazed to even stand on my own feet. I realized that I had missed out on an opportunity that I would never get back.'

Dutt says he tried every drug in the book. But he developed a particular addiction to cocaine and heroin. Once Nargis realized that her son might be on drugs, she asked Zaheeda, her niece, to speak to him about the habit. Zaheeda took him out for ice cream and asked him if he was on drugs. Dutt denied it. But she warned him that his mother was aware of his addiction. 'You think she cannot see it but she knows what's eating you up inside,' she told him.

At a chat hosted by the Federation of Indian Chambers of Commerce and Industry's Ladies Organization, Sanjay recounted a particularly horrific incident during the making of *Rocky*. 'I remember that I was so addicted that once I travelled with a kilogram of heroin hidden in my shoes. My two sisters were also with me on the same flight. At that time, checking at airports was not so strict. Today, when I think about the incident, I get scared. *Main pakda jaata toh theek tha* (If I got caught, it would be fine), but what about my sisters? Drugs do this to you. You don't care about family or anything else.'

After *Rocky*, Sanjay's drug addiction had peaked. One day, he woke up from a heroin binge and began to look for something to eat. The domestic help told him, 'Baba, you've slept for two days straight. Everyone in the house has gone mad with worry.' Sanjay looked at his face in the mirror, went to his father's room and said, 'Dad, I am dying. You have to save me.' He was first taken to the Breach Candy Hospital Detox Center and then to a rehab centre in Texas. Sunil Dutt, being the conscientious person that he was, informed all the producers that his son was an addict and that until and unless he cleaned up his act he was not coming back.

Dutt was sent to the same place that had treated his mother: Sloan and Kettering. The road to recovery was a slow and painful one. And it lasted for over eight months.

When he was asked if he started doing drugs again because his mother, Nargis, passed away, Dutt said, in an interview to *The Times of India*, 'It's not that I started because of mom. *Mera dog mar gaya toh daaru pi raha hoon, aaj mera gadha mar gaya to daaru piyunga* (I am drinking because my dog has died, I will drink because my donkey died today)—these are just excuses. Substance abuse is something that you do if you want to do it. Once you get into it, it's very difficult to leave. It is the worst thing in the world. My journey with substance abuse lasted for about twelve years. There are no drugs in the world that I have not done. When my father took me to America (to the rehab centre), they gave me a list (of drugs) and I ticked every drug on it—because I had taken all of them. The doctor told my dad, "What kind of food do you eat in India? Going by the drugs he did, he should be dead by now!"'

Dutt confessed he did not quit drugs because of his family. 'I left because I wanted to be out of it. I didn't want that life. When you start the rehabilitation process, one part is physical—your body breaks down and you feel cold. But the most difficult part comes later, when your mind says, "*Ab toh tu theek ho gaya hai, ek baar maar lete hain* (now you're fixed, let's just do it one more time)." That's when you have to use willpower.' Since he got clean, and was cleared of all charges in the long-drawn legal cases, he has been a regular at anti-drug panel discussions, where he tells youngsters, 'Live your life, love your work, love your family. It is better than cocaine.'

Sanjay Dutt may not have spoken the truth on every occasion. He may have hidden some facts. But when it comes to his addiction, even his fiercest critics will tell you that he is brutally honest.

Post rehab, Dutt was a lot more at peace with himself. Reports began emerging in film magazines that he had struck up a friendship with a cattle rancher named Bill. He had invested in a long horn cattle ranch of his own; he was in the midst of nature, building a new life for himself. He had bought a small flat in New York and was planning to run a steakhouse in the city. However, two months later, Sunil Dutt flew down to meet him. He wanted his son to come back. Sanjay didn't want to return; he didn't want to do films. But his father pleaded, and eventually, despite all the years of resentment, misunderstanding, angst and hurt, Sanjay gave in.

Back in India, everyone had written off the prodigal son—the charsi, the addict, who had brought shame to the Dutt family. But in the first of many 'comebacks' that were to follow, the fresh-from-the-American-farm Sanjay devoted his energy to sculpting his body and starred in *Naam*, one of the biggest hits of 1986.

4

In the Name of the Father

'Sons have always a rebellious wish to be disillusioned by that which charmed their fathers'

—Aldous Huxley

History says star-sons have always played hopscotch with their fathers' legacies. Sanjay Dutt was no exception. While his devotion toward his mother has been well established, not enough has been documented about how he spent his childhood living in the shadow of a father who, in modern parlance, would be described as tyrannical.

This may be incomprehensible for those who remember Sunil Dutt as the stately gentleman; the soft-spoken, kind-hearted, earnest and upright citizen; the social worker and devoted husband. But even the finest of men and husbands do not always make the best of fathers.

The world would not come to know about what really went on in the Dutt household, had it not been for a sensational interview of Sanjay Dutt by *Stardust* many moons ago, which first seeded the idea that his reckless, self-destructive behaviour was probably a result of bad parenting.

It was just the kind of fodder that the entertainment media of early '90s needed to create and perpetuate the myth that was Dutt. Here was a prodigal son, lashing out against the father with an impeccable public image, saying things like, 'It wasn't as if my father didn't love me, but he chose to express his feelings in a strange way so that I can never get myself to talk to dad the way my sister Priya can. They share a different rapport altogether. Priya has always been dad's favourite. Of course, my dad and I are friendlier now. If I have a problem, I can go and tell him about it, but it has taken a long time, a very long time to reach that stage. It's very strange that even after becoming a father myself, I am still looking for dad's approval. He treats me like a kid even today. He is forever reprimanding me and I am still reacting. I know I should have been used to his behaviour by now, but I am not. I guess some things between us will never change.'

Dutt claimed he was always scared of his father because the latter was quite forceful—a strict disciplinarian. 'Whenever I think of childhood, I am filled with fear... deep fear,' he said to *Stardust*.

He spoke of an incident when he was only six years old. He had started using foul language and the dirtiest of cuss words liberally at the domestic helps. One day, one of them complained to his father. A furious Sunil Dutt dragged Sanju to his room, took out his belt and lashed him. When Nargis heard his screams, she ran in to save him. 'If she hadn't, dad would have probably beaten me black and blue that day,' said Dutt. The good cop–bad cop routine took its toll on the precocious boy.

On the one hand, his father couldn't see beyond his faults and on the other hand, his mother was almost completely blind to them—and they both blamed each other for a common crime. Sanjay spoke of another incident: as a child, he was petrified of water. But Sunil Dutt wanted him to swim. He recounted to the journalist, 'He (dad) picked me up one day and threw me into the pool and kept pushing my head into the water while I gasped and struggled like crazy. "Now will you learn swimming?" dad asked me later. And within the next two days, I had learnt to swim. The purpose was served but there was a cost he had paid unknowingly. His weird ways of teaching me had infuriated me even more.'

And then there was the smoking incident. 'He felt that I had gone out of control and as punishment, sent me away to boarding school. My mother was frantic but her tears failed to make my father change his mind. That was the turning point of my life.' He revealed to the same magazine.

The rift between Sanjay Dutt and his father would widen years later, when the prodigal son was in his early twenties—and deep into what would be known as the Tina Munim affair.

*

Fresh out of college, Sanjay had started dating Tina Munim, a fresh-faced girl from a wealthy Gujarati family with stars in her eyes. Sunil Dutt had been against this relationship; he wanted his son to focus on his work instead. It was during this time that Sanjay, who had been out—presumably working till late at night—came home early in the morning, only to find that he had been locked out. His father had instructed the family, especially Nargis, to keep him out. Sunil Dutt suspected, not without reason perhaps, that his son was still hanging out with Tina—even after being instructed to avoid her beyond professional reasons. When Sanjay saw the locked door, he threw a fit. His style. Nargis rushed out and pleaded with Dutt sahab to let him in. But the father was adamant. He gave her an ultimatum—*it's either me or him*. Predictably, Nargis chose her son over her husband. An infuriated Sunil Dutt drove away and did not come back for the rest of the day—or the night. Later, the family found out that he was with a bunch of his friends in the outskirts of the city. This was one of the many incidents that damaged the awkward father-son relationship.

For the longest time, Dutt blamed his father's parenting methods for his waywardness, projecting himself as the victim. His mother's death didn't help either. All his life, his parents were always at loggerheads when it came to the son. And while Sanjay had grown closer to his mother, he could never get over the fact that his father had pushed him away from his only place of love and compassion, pushing him deeper into the cycle of addiction, relapse and denial. It was only when a doctor at his rehab made him listen to the audio tapes of his mother's voice during her last stages—addressing him when he was away—that he broke down and cried. The floodgates had opened.

Something else happened too. It was his sister Namrata aka Anju's marriage. Sanjay, in an interview to *Stardust* claimed: 'Not that I was against it—it's just that I couldn't come to terms with the idea of my sister having a boyfriend. When I was kind of getting accustomed, dad came and told me that he had fixed her wedding. I was furious because I had been completely left out of the picture. It was a major decision and I had not even been intimated, forget consulted with. I felt very slighted and I told dad that the marriage would have to wait until I got back from the States. But I didn't feel like coming back after I was cured. There was nothing left for me in India. I felt it would be better if I settled down in the States itself, but dad wanted me to come back. He assured me that things would become better. But the minute I landed in India, dad washed his hands off me. Here I was with the reputation of being a drug addict behind me, expected to resurrect my career with no help or cooperation from anywhere. I felt very let down. I had come back because of dad and he was suddenly behaving so strangely. I was damn pissed off. I felt like a fool. No producer wanted me. I had no work, because no one wanted to touch me with a barge pole. Not even my dad. Even he refused to make a film with me.'

The already tenuous relationship between father and son was severely tested at this point. When Sanjay left for the US for drug rehab, the family was also going through a major crisis. It wasn't as though they had stopped caring for him. It was just that they were all grieving and hurting in their own ways and coping with

Nargis', death—the loss that had ripped their lives apart. So, after eight months of despair, Sanjay starred in *Jaan Ki Baazi* (1985) opposite Anita Raj—his first release post rehab. Action director Pappu Verma turned producer with this film and Ajay Kashyap, erstwhile assistant to filmmaker Narendra Bedi, made his debut as director. *Jaan Ki Baazi,* Sanjay's comeback film, was successful.

This typical 'girl meets boy till tragedy strikes and vengeance is unleashed' film was followed by a string of flops: *Bekaraar, Johnny I Love You* and *Mera Faisla*. But then came *Naam* and Dutt was back in the reckoning.

'Maybe what my dad did was a blessing in disguise,' a mellow Sanjay reflected in the course of a *Stardust* interview later on. 'Perhaps he had meant it that way—that I should pick myself up on my own so I could value my career and success even more. Sometimes I feel awkward expressing myself to dad. Even he feels the same way when it comes to praising me.'

In a way, it took Sanjay a long time to confront his own feelings about his father and get over his fear and misgivings. He spoke of another incident in another *Stardust* interview: 'When my sister Anju left her in-laws' place and came to live with us with her husband, dad didn't like it. Not because he didn't want them to stay with us, but because he didn't want to encourage any further problems between her in-laws and her. But I put my foot down. She is my sister and I was not going to let her cry. And for once dad had no option but to give in.'

Time and again, there were flashpoints in their relationship when Sunil and Sanjay Dutt would be pitted against each other.

While they sparred over family matters, the Dutt family always rallied around the prodigal son when the time came. However, Sanjay's relationship with Priya Dutt was complicated by the fact that he always thought of her as her father's favourite, and she always saw him as the mollycoddled one. She thought of him as the one who got the family into trouble time and again. She allegedly resented the fact that he betrayed his father's ideals and Congress party roots by joining their nemesis Samajwadi Party (headed by Mulayam Singh Yadav and fronted by Amar Singh, who was known to Yield tremendous influence over Bollywood and UP heavyweights such as Subrata Roy of Sahara), as well as seeking out Shiv Sena Supremo Balasaheb Thackeray's blessings when he was in jail. Yet their bonds ran deep and strong enough to survive these pulls and tremors.

Sanjay was concerned about the fact that more than anything else, he felt compelled to seek his father's approval till very late in life. That his father was not exactly a generous person when it came to praise or public displays of love and affection, affected him. He knew he was his mother's blue-eyed boy but his craving for his father's validation and approval tormented him to no end. He said in the same *Stardust* interview: 'I know, I know he loves me. It's just that he refuses to take me seriously. When I told him that I wanted to marry Richa, he just laughed at me and asked me—are you really serious? I had to literally be after him to talk to Richa's parents. I don't think he had much faith in my decision. For some reason, he has always reacted very negatively towards my girlfriends. He never liked any of them. Of course I did not expect him to start treating Richa like a daughter immediately after marriage. Neither did I expect her to start treating him like a father. It takes time for people to adjust to each other but Richa's illness had changed everything. And through her illness and the various operations, dad was by my side. But he did not help me take any decisions. He left that to me. It was just for me to take those major decisions about Richa by my own and I am happy that I am capable of looking after my life and my child and taking decisions for them.'

When the time came, the father did not abandon the child. The family did not abandon the prodigal son. Dutt said to the same publication, 'Dad will be dad. When he heard that *Thanedaar* was going well, he came and hugged me. He was happy for me. And that's the best he can express. He is made the way he is and I guess it's difficult for him to change now. But he is trying of course. That doesn't mean that he has stopped fighting with me. He hates my hairstyle, got freaked out when I got my hair cut and spiked and was furious when I got my ears pierced. But that's him. At least he is making an attempt today. We sometimes feel that when things are out of control we can go and at least talk to him. And these days he listens. He pays heed to what we say and tries to make amends, to the extent he can, of course.'

Even if Sanju never idolized his father as a child, he thought that he had become more like his father over the years. 'I wanted to be everything he was not… I wanted to give all the freedom to my children. I wanted to be a lenient and indulgent father. But today I realize that I am just an extension of him. As a husband and a father, I am just him. Sometimes when I say something or do something, I suddenly realize and I tell myself—shit, that's him. And he is probably right.' According to him, if you look at his relationship with his firstborn, Trishala, over the years, you will see in him merely a different version of Sunil Dutt.

Sunil Dutt—minus the virtues that made him Sunil Dutt.

The reason Sanjay was not supportive of Trishala getting into the glamour business or the film industry, or any part of the world that he belonged to, was that he was overprotective. What he was looking for in the women he chose to marry was essentially a homemaker—a 'sahadharmini', like his mother was to his father. Somebody who would be at home for him and perhaps take care of the household and cook and sew and make flowers grow, as Dylan would have sung. He didn't really want a career woman. He may have dated several women from the industry, but ultimately he wanted someone far more domesticated. And Nargis, for all her stardom and all her fame and all her success, was something of a domesticated person herself.

It is worth noting that this father–son relationship was recreated in a film that was a major milestone in Sanjay Dutt's career: Rajkumar Hirani's *Munna Bhai M.B.B.S.*

Released in 2003, *Munna Bhai M.B.B.S.* was inspired by the 1998 Hollywood film, *Patch Adams*. It involves the protagonist, the Mumbai don Munna Bhai (Dutt), going to a medical school with the help of his sidekick Circuit (Arshad Warsi). It also starred Jimmy Shergill, Gracy Singh, Boman Irani and Sunil Dutt. Sunil and Sanjay

Dutt acted together after a decade in this film. Though they had appeared earlier in *Reshma Aur Shera*, *Rocky* and *Kshatriya* (1993), Sunil Dutt returned to the screen after a hiatus of ten years to play Munna's father. Although Shah Rukh Khan was originally cast as Munna, with Sanjay Dutt as Circuit—and Vivek Oberoi was also considered for the role—it was perhaps providence that Sanjay Dutt eventually took the role of Munna, which ultimately gave him an image makeover and helped change the public perception of this controversial superstar.

The father–son relationship turned out to be one of the biggest talking points in the film. It was significant on many different levels. It came at a point when Sanjay Dutt's professional (and personal) currency was at its lowest. For years, there had been an unspoken wave of sympathy that he had been riding—for being 'rudderless' since his mother's death and perpetually nursing a broken heart. But in 2003, it was no longer working. He was under the scanner for his widely reported terror links and his marriage to Rhea Pillai was on the rocks. It was time for a reinvention—and Rajkumar Hirani provided the perfect opportunity. The poor boy missing his mother was now the poor boy failing to live up to his father's expectations. This pitch hit the sweet spot with the audiences. So far, the Hindi film audience had been used to films with fathers and sons locked in ideological conflicts over power, politics or love. The other extreme was the son avenging his father's death and/or humiliation. This was perhaps the first time that they saw, on-screen, a son and a father who had love for each other but were unable to see what they really had in common. They saw a son constantly seeking his father's approval, and failing. The obvious parallels with Dutt's real life were what worked for the movie, where Munna spends close to two hours trying to make his father smile by changing himself and the world.

Circuit's subplot is also relevant. As several film critics pointed out, the sidekick trope was not just meant to evoke laughter. He was Munna, minus the physical stature. A puppy for whom his boss was Napoleon. Here was a lackey who would do anything to make Munna smile. To him, aggression and violence come easy, and the audience is willing to overlook the gory details because he seems to have a pure heart and the purest intent. He revels in his role—that of a facilitator for his beloved Munna. The latter understands this, appreciates it and gives Circuit his space, even empowering him by putting him in charge when he is away redeeming himself in medical school. The fact that he does not want his friend to change, even when he is transforming his own life, says something about how Sanjay viewed this relationship between a father figure and a protégé. Even when he does not really say 'thank you', he makes it evident that he is deeply grateful to Circuit. In his interactions with Circuit you can also hear Sanjay pleading with his father to be generous, forgiving, accepting and appreciative. To rescue him from feeling unloved.

In the film, Sunil Dutt finally accepts Munna for what he is—even after all hopes of medical school are wiped out with a 'jadoo ki jhappi'. In real life, too, after two decades of playing gangster roles and hanging out with gangsters while his father continued to be a person with tremendous moral rectitude, Sunil Dutt finally approved of his son's choices.

Sanjay has said, in subsequent interviews, that the characters of his parents in the film were modelled on his own parents, who were true Gandhians in spirit. We know that Sunil Dutt was a strict disciplinarian and given to a certain kind of tough behaviour, but it is not difficult to understand where it came from. In an interview with rediff.com, director Rajkumar Hirani said, '[Sunil Dutt] came [in] very prepared. He used to call me and say, "Give me my lines in Urdu." He reads in Urdu script. So we did that. When he walked onto the set he knew his lines, left, right and center. He is a nice guy. You can communicate with him. Even if you ask him to redo a take ten times, it's okay. The problem was with other actors. When Boman Irani walked in, he was absolutely nervous... He got nervous, because Dutt was working in a film after sixteen years. Arshad Warsi was nervous on the first day of shooting as well. Of course, all that was solved within two days.'

There were health issues as well with Dutt sahab. 'He had a problem in his shoulder. There was a scene where he had to hug Sanjay Dutt. I called for action and he didn't move. We cut the camera. I said action again. We realized he couldn't move his arms. Sanjay was extremely worried. He said, "Pack up, let's take him to the hospital." But Sunil Dutt insisted he would finish the shot. He sat down for a while, had a cup of tea and got back. I knew he was in pain but he insisted. He lifted his hand with great effort. When you watch that shot, remember he was in great pain. It is this old school discipline that I feel I should imbibe from these people. How they can go through any type of pain and still work?'

Speaking about the tender father-son moment in the film,

Hirani said, 'You see them hugging in the film. I get emotional about the whole thing whenever I think of it. Do you hug your mom or dad often? I don't know how many times Sanjay has hugged his father. So that whole hugging scene, hugging each other, it was real. They probably hugged after, I don't know how many years. It is so real.'

'Jadu ki jhappi' became a national rage. It became a popular catchphrase, an idea that spread like wildfire. In its essence, it is such a simple thing—just making an effort to show your love for somebody, be it an estranged father, an adoring mother, or just a sweeper whose services you always take for granted but who you never really appreciate. It was like Sanjay Dutt's life had come full circle. For the emotionally stunted Sanju, *Munna Bhai M.B.B.S.* was like a 'jadu ki jhappi'—the warm, affectionate miracle hug that changed everything.

Given his own complex relationship with his father, did Sanjay Dutt do things any differently with his firstborn, Trishala?

Dutt's controversial personal and professional life was the perfect backdrop for the media to speculate on the tumultuous relationship he shared with Trishala, who, it was believed, had been brought up to hate him. And not without reason.

In interviews that appeared over the years, Trishala and Dutt both denied the strain in their bond. But the fact is, she had been kept away from her father by her maternal grandparents and had given many a nasty interview about him. The script started changing somewhere down the line. In an interview with *Hindustan Times*, Trishala explained the peculiar circumstances of her early life: 'I never accompany dad to any filmy parties because I am barely in Mumbai to begin with…when I am in Mumbai I spend time with dad and Manyata because I haven't seen them in so long. I faced a lot of challenges growing up and till today I face new challenges everyday but I always find a way to fix them. Unlike other star kids, I don't have the luxury to have mommy and daddy help with things. I don't have the luxury of a father to "make a phone call" or "pull a favour" for me as the others do. It's hard with no help and you have to do everything on your own.' Trishala eventually took the Indian media to task for misrepresenting the relationship between her father and her, claiming that they had hardly been out of the tabloids since Sanjay started dating Manyata in 2007.

Soon, as news broke of Dutt marrying Manyata, who was only six years older than his daughter, it opened a floodgate of gossip and speculation fuelled by reports that the daughter was not taking the father's calls. Trishala denied this in an interview with *People* magazine. 'No, I wasn't ignoring his calls, I was busy… There were times when I was in class when dad called and then it would be too late for me to call him back in India. Dad got the wrong idea of why I wasn't taking his calls so he finally SMSed me and I called him back.' In the same interview, she said, 'I spoke to my father few weeks after his marriage. It was like any other conversation, completely normal. There was no tension between us.' The journalist noted that in 'the days preceding their meeting, Trishala was both nervous and happy, nervous because she had met her dad after over one and a half years. Joyous because she was looking forward to spending some quality time with him. It is clear that it was a very emotional six days for both father and daughter, they connected with each other once again. As for Trishala and Manyata, it will be interesting to see how the relationship develops. While Trishala's only wish is to see her father happy, 6 days is too soon for anyone to save a conviction whether she and Manyata will go on to forge a meaningful relationship.'

One would imagine this friction or tension between the father and daughter was perhaps just a case of a child being possessive about a father she barely knew. It was intensified when Trishala, who seemed to share her father's propensity to shoot his mouth, spoke to the media about how she was 'the only woman' in his life.

Eventually, Dutt's first born and his third wife got along swimmingly. Trishala abandoned her plans for a Bollywood career—something that Dutt had always disapproved of. She has found her calling in fashion design and entrepreneurship. Meanwhile, Manyata has been busy being the new Mrs Dutt, matriarch of the family.

5

Lowering the Bar

'When I saw them put the handcuffs on my son for the first time, I felt as though all the work I had done in my life, for my country, had come to nothing. I was about to break down when Sanjay, realising my anguish, patted my arm and said, "Relax dad, it is okay, part of the procedure."'

—Sunil Dutt to Simi Garewal on *Rendezvous with Simi*

'There are a lot of unanswered questions about the Bombay Blasts,' said Dutt to veteran journalist Shoma Chaudhury at an open session in Delhi, post his release from jail. 'Most people do not even remember or ask why calls were made from the Mantralaya to Dawood Ibrahim, how so much RDX could be moved around in the city, right under the noses of the cops… But all people remember is Sanjay Dutt.'

Today, Dutt can afford to be openly critical of the system that cast its long and sinister shadow on his life for twenty-three years. Today, he can taunt the Joint Commissioner of Police at the time of his arrest, M.N. Singh, calling him names ('he is more interested in acting... and blabber on TV' in the same interview). Being a man free of the charges of abetting and colluding with terrorists gives you the confidence and audacity to do so. Today, Dutt can hold his own, discussing the minutae of the legal cases that he had to fight for over two decades. But things were quite different when he was in the thick of it.

It perhaps started with the riots that ravaged Mumbai post the demolition of the Babri Masjid. Sunil Dutt, a parliamentarian and a humanitarian, was on the streets, helping those affected by the rioting and the looting. According to Sanjay Dutt, this somehow created the impression that his father was 'pro-Muslim'. It could have been because of his wife, it could have been because of his political leaning, but in those volatile days, word of mouth killed more people than the enemy's sword.

Sanjay has said in several televised interviews since then (BBC, Shoma Chaudhury) that the family began to receive threat calls. His sister, Priya, was in college at the time. The family's requests for police protection were repeatedly turned down.

Those were also the days when the underworld called the shots in the film industry. Quite literally. Films were funded by the mafia and stars were obliged to make appearances at events hosted by gangsters—especially in Dubai. Said Sanjay, 'It was at this time that a producer asked me if I wanted a gun...' One casual remark led to another and the star, who was then at a professional high with a gym-fresh sculpted body and a string of commercial successes, suddenly had an AK-47 in his hands. A fact he has admitted to, repeatedly, but always defending his intent-self preservation and protecting his family.

But that was not all. Dutt was accused of accepting a delivery of weapons at his house from notorious gangster Abu Salem and his co-accused Riaz Siddiqui, who had also been implicated in the blasts. It was claimed that the weapons formed a part of a large consignment of arms connected to the terror masterminds.

In April 1993, Dutt was shooting in Mauritius, when his sister Priya called him up to inform him that there were reports that he had three illegal weapons at home. True to his nature, he shrugged it off. But once he landed at the Mumbai airport and looked at the posse of policemen waiting for him, it hit him.

In Sanjay's own words (from the Shoma Chaudhury interview), M.N. Singh initially assured him that he would be let off lightly under the more forgiving Arms Possession Act. The words that he reportedly used were, '*baccha hai, galti ho gaya*... *papa se baat kar liya* (you're a kid, you've made a mistake... I've talked to your father).' Within hours, however, Singh claimed that he had been 'instructed' to slap the more stringent Terrorist and Disruptive Activities Prevention Act (TADA) on Sanjay and have him arrested in connection with the Bomb Blast case. 'That is when I fell at his feet,' said Sanjay.

The judge rejected his defence—protection for his family—and also refused bail. Dutt went back to jail at Arthur Road and was soon moved to Yerwada Central Jail in Pune. He was granted bail by the Supreme Court in 1995 but was rearrested in December the same year and released on bail in April 1997. He had a bit of a respite from 1997 till 2006, when the case came to court. In 2006–07, he spent seven months in Arthur Road jail and Pune prison on three occasions. He appealed against the sentence and was granted interim bail on 20 August 2007. On 22 October 2007, Dutt was back in jail and applied for bail once again. On 27 November 2007, he was granted bail by the Supreme Court and on 21 March, 2013, the Supreme Court upheld the verdict of the TADA court but shortened the sentence to five years of imprisonment. Dutt was given a month to surrender before the authorities.

Eventually, Abdul Qayum Abdul Karim Sheikh, a close associate of Dawood Ibrahim, was arrested. Dutt had reportedly given Qayum's name to the police, saying that in September 1992, he had bought a pistol from Qayum in Dubai.

On 31 July 2007, the TADA court sentenced Dutt to six years of rigorous imprisonment for illegal possession of weapons and cleared him of charges relating to the blasts. For Dutt, it was a moment of triumph. The stain of terror, of being a 'deshdrohi (treasonist)' was finally off his life. Possessing illegal arms was the lesser evil in his lexicon.

A reporter working with some of the leading city newspapers, Anand Holla, offered a ringside view of the court's proceedings, which he said marked a 'crucial moment in India's judicial history.' In a piece written for *Arré (global)*, Holla recalled that day in 2007 when Dutt's life hung in the balance once again. Those were the heady days post-Munna Bhai. And the success of the films had stirred fan loyalties. But the wave of affection and sympathy stopped short of the walls of the TADA court. Describing Dutt's demeanour during the court hearings, Holla wrote,

> In a quiet corner by the discoloured metal stairs that swirled upward, Dutt, dapper in his staple attire of a full-sleeved blue shirt with three buttons undone, denims, tapering boots, a fistful of gold chains, and hand-swept hair, grew mildly animated upon my mention of his blockbuster. 'You know, kids love Circuit way more than they love Munna Bhai. I have a live example in my family,' he said, chuckling, his head tilted to the side. [...]
>
> 'It is strange,' he continued. 'I am obviously happy about *Lage Raho*'s success, but I also have no idea what the judgment will be. It's a different world here...'
>
> A few weeks after this exchange, Judge Pramod Kode handed out an emphatic clean chit straight out of a simplistic movie sequence—'You are not a terrorist'—and a cascade of sweet relief swept over Dutt's sweat-speckled face.

According to those who had followed the star, including Holla, he was rather unremarkable inside the court—'unpretentious' and displaying a certain 'naiveté', sometimes even to the point of not caring. He would sometimes regale the accompanying journalists with trivia from his life on the set, where he belonged. Holla recalls how he once told him: 'Dancing is tough for me...when David (Dhawan) asked me to do these ridiculous dances abroad, like in

Europe, it got so embarrassing, I'd tell David, "*Ab bas bhi karo, Sir* (Let's stop now, sir)!"'

There was more. Sometimes Dutt would saunter in, droopy shoulders, robotic stride. '...unmistakably inebriated, his heaving breath betraying whiskey. He'd empty sachets of Manikchand gutkha, and if you caught his eye, he'd just wink at you and chomp away,' wrote Holla.

All reporters covering the trial agree that despite the seemingly vice-like grip of the legal cases, Dutt always got away with way too many exemptions from appearances. His busy shoot schedules and his lawyer were always handy. Even during his incarceration between 1993 and 1995, when there were stories about the hardships he faced in prison, Holla says he had his way around certain things. Apparently, 'a special coconut oil was called for, to nourish his long mane; regular coconut water in polythene pouches to soothe his damaged kidneys. The fact that he would pour the latter in a steel glass and take endless little sips from it while munching on packaged snacks convinced at least some reporters that the coconut water was mixed with something more robust...like vodka.' Just like the old stories about Dutt drinking the blood of a freshly slaughtered reptile just for a dare, this, too, hovered between myth and reality. Like everything else in his life.

There was a time when Sunil Dutt, who had fought like a lion to keep his son out of jail, had to come to terms with the fact that he had failed. His political party, the Congress, failed him. There were whispers about how the party heavyweights had kept him waiting for hours and refused to grant him an audience. And that his public empathy for the minorities was something that the present disposition was not comfortable with. It was a huge blow to the parliamentarian, who had spent a lifetime serving his people and his party.

Then, one day, Sunil Dutt visited his son in prison, and broke down. 'I am sorry, son. I cannot help you anymore.'

6

Strange Bedfellows

It does not take an Einstein to figure out that politics and Sanjay Dutt don't mix. Dutt sahab was revered as a social activist, a humanitarian whose work with the homeless and the downtrodden is one of his finest legacies. He and Nargis, as MPs, were the first stars to actually go to the border to lift the morale of the soldiers. It became fashionable for Bollywood stars to promote their films by dancing and singing with the soldiers much later on. But when Mrs and Mr Dutt did it, decades ago, they had no film to promote and neither were they espousing any political ideology. Dutt sahab immersed himself in social work post Nargis's death and it was his party that benefitted from his exemplary work on the streets. Priya Dutt followed him closely. And yet, when the time came, the party evidently threw him under the wheels. Even then, the stately parliamentarian and humanitarian never spoke ill of his party. Not in public, at least. He was a living example of how a truly evolved soul seeks nothing more than the courage to change what he can and the grace to accept what he cannot.

When Sanjay's drug problems surfaced, Sunil Dutt was younger, stronger and more surefooted in the world of movies. He could actually tell the producers that his son was an addict and had nothing to hide from the world. But the terror taint shook him to the core and ripped him apart. It was the classic fight between duty and love—a battle between the head and the heart. Such was his image that people were willing to give Sanjay a clean chit, simply because he was fighting for his son. Even if the world wasn't sure of Dutt's involvement in the blasts, they knew Sunil Dutt was not a dishonest man—and all he was asking for, was forgiveness. His public stance was somewhere in between—he was not defending his son's actions, neither was he walking away from him. He was simply being a father, pleading with the system to show leniency towards his star-crossed son. But politics had no place for an honest man's biggest weakness.

For Sanjay, however, politics was about ever-changing loyalties, shifting goalposts and a matter of convenience. And it had everything to do with twenty-three years of being on the wrong side of the law.

When his options were running out, someone counselled the family to try a different approach. Dutt sahab and his son met with Balasaheb Thackeray. It was irony playing itself out with all the flourish of a Hindi film script. Here was the man who had an alleged role in the communal riots that changed Mumbai forever. He was the embodiment of everything that Sunil and Nargis Dutt had fought

In Rocky *(1981)*

With Sunny Deol

With Rajendra Kumar and Priya Dutt

With Yash Chopra

With Kumar Gaurav

With Anita Raj

With Pooja Bhatt

With Anil Kapoor

With Dilip Kumar

With Sridevi

With Shatrughan Sinha and Jackie Shroff

With Jaya Bachchan

With Ramesh Sippy

With Simi Garewal

Sanjay Dutt, standing out

Sanjay Dutt, the 'bad boy'

With Rahul Roy and Mahesh Bhatt

With Saroj Khan and Shah Rukh Khan

With Padmini Kolhapuri

With his father Sunil Dutt and sisters Priya and Namrata

With his mother Nargis

With Subhash Ghai and Kumar Gaurav

Sanjay Dutt celebrating his birthday with friends

With Salman Khan

With Madhuri Dixit

With his parents Sunil Dutt and Nargis

against, ideologically and practically. And yet, with their back to the wall, father and son were genuflecting before him. To Shoma Chaudhury, Sanjay defended that controversial decision saying that the late Supremo was fond of his mother and considered her to be his sister. He claimed that the late Thackeray and Sunil Dutt were actually good friends, despite their political and ideological cleft. And once Thackeray had placed his rudraksh-wrapped hand on Sanjay's troubled and star-crossed head, a number of doors opened up.

Veteran journalist Aakar Patel, who was also among the posse of media persons on Dutt's case, said: 'Sanjay's luck changed when the Shiv Sena came to power in Maharashtra's assembly elections of 1995. Bal Thackeray leaned on the Centre to let the CBI, which was prosecuting, relax its opposition to bail… When Sanjay got bail, he went to thank Thackeray and then to Siddhi Vinayak temple.' Sanjay, sporting a blazing saffron tika, was heard saying around this time, 'I am grateful to Balasaheb Thackeray. He has been a huge influence.'

His son's legal trouble began affecting Dutt sahab's political career. The five-time MP had contested his first Lok Sabha election after joining the Congress in 1984 and won the Mumbai North West seat in his maiden attempt. He retained it in the 1989 and 1991 elections but did not contest the 1996 and 1998 elections. It was only after Sanjay Dutt was out on bail in 1997 that Dutt sahab returned to his grass-roots work and won the 1999, 2000 and 2004 elections. He passed away in 2005 in his sleep at his residence after suffering a heatstroke while travelling in the interiors of the country for work.

In 2006, the TADA court verdict freed Sanjay from the terror link charges. He only had to deal with the monkey on his back—the arms possession case. But Sanjay's destiny continued to play snakes and ladders with him and the following year, he was rearrested and taken to Yerwada prison, where, after eighteen days, he managed to get bail.

Without his father to anchor his life and steer him away from danger, Sanjay was ripe for the plucking. Nudged by some of the most powerful Bollywood families of the time, he began inching towards political heavyweight, influencer and networker Amar Singh. Within a couple of years, he had campaigned for Singh's companion and SP candidate Jaya Prada in Uttar Pradesh. In 2008, when he married Manyata, Amar Singh and Jaya Prada apparently did their bit to ensure that the contested marriage was given its due sanction. In 2009, he gave a sensational interview to a news channel. 'My father died because of Congress... they (Congress) did not listen to him, such a senior leader... and took Sanjay Nirupam in Congress, the man who accused him, the man who abused him when he (Nirupam) was in Shiv Sena. He died because of that,' he said in his usual blustering style. 'He spoke to me four days before he died. The only hurt he had was this. He told me they (Congress) had killed him.' It did not stop at that. Asked to comment on his sister Priya Dutt's association with Congress, for which she is an MP, he said, 'To be with the party which killed her father... that is her choice.'

'If they valued my father so much, at least they could have loved me a little bit,' Dutt said, clarifying at the same time, however, that he was not saying that Congress should have helped him. In 2009, spurning the overtures from Congress party, Dutt chose to align himself with the SP officially. He received the party ticket for the Lucknow Lok Sabha constituency, a decision that proved to be ill-advised.

Priya Dutt, always the most outspoken of the Dutt kids, made it evident that Dutt had 'disgraced' the family. 'For the first time since he died I am thankful he is no longer alive to see this ignominy,' she reportedly told *Hindustan Times*, attacking Manyata as well in the process. Priya apparently alleged that Dutt's ambition was an extension of his wife's. The media had a field day when Dutt, in his usual style, rose to the bait. He made politically incorrect statements on 'how a woman shouldn't keep her father's surname after her marriage' and how 'no sister gets along with her brother's wife'; and that the only true Mr and Mrs Dutt, inheritors of the Sunil Dutt–Nargis legacy, were he and Manyata, not Priya.

In a particularly juicy piece in *Outlook India*, the Dutt family feud was said to have been designed by Manyata and Amar Singh. For the beleaguered new wife, Jaya Prada was a solid support system. In fact, when Dutt's candidature was announced, Jaya Prada urged people to vote for Manyata in case the Supreme Court decided to sentence him.

The article said that Manyata had changed Dutt's 'inner circle entirely, wrenched him away from family and friends who have stood by him through his years of waywardness, drug addiction and imprisonment.'

Citing the examples of his former buddies, filmmakers Sanjay

Gupta and Mahesh Manjrekar, who were now persona non grata, the writer said:

> Manyata, who also manages Sanjay's film production business, says she has brought responsibility and stability into Sanjay's life and has defended her decision to keep his so-called friends at bay. 'There were too many people trying to use him. I came like a barricade between him and those who wanted to use him.'
>
> However, the instability is still evident in Sanjay's see-sawing on his entry into politics, his stance shifting by the day, from 'I am always there for Soniaji and Rahulji,' to 'I am disappointed with the Congress. It was not there for me in my hour of need,' to thanking Digvijay Singh for standing by him, and dithering about whether he would contest from Lucknow against A.B. Vajpayee.
>
> What is becoming increasingly evident is that it's more Manyata's decision than his own. At the recent *Hindustan Times* summit, while Sanjay was evasive about entering politics, it was Manyata, sitting in the audience, who declared he should and he will (join politics) when *HT* advisory editorial director Vir Sanghvi directed the question at her. Her political ambitions were also evident when she led the peace march at the Gateway after the terror attacks. 'She wants to be an MP's wife and achieve her own goals by keeping her hold on him,' says an insider, who adds that it was also Manyata's way of getting even with Priya, who had assumed Sunil Dutt's political mantle.

When he did arrive in Lucknow, Dutt was greeted with black flags and posters of AK-47s. But he put up a brave front. The SP had offered him a lifeline when he desperately needed to leverage his Munna Bhai image and earn a reprise from the apex court. His career, too, was in the doldrums.

But, somehow, even Singh's magic did not quite work on Dutt's sinking fortunes—especially at a time when Singh himself was being sidelined in the party, which had touched giddying heights thanks to his networking prowess. In 2010, Dutt withdrew his candidature.

Explaining his decision to withdraw from electoral politics, Dutt said told reporters, 'I am not a politician but I belong to a political family.' He said he was persuaded by a close friend to contest the 2009 Lok Sabha elections as a candidate for the SP, but withdrew, when the court refused to suspend the conviction. He was then appointed General Secretary of the party, and he left the post in December 2010. A year later, expressing sadness over the way his 'mentor' Amar Singh was treated in the party, Sanjay resigned from the post and subsequently quit the party.

Speaking to the media after his political misadventures, Dutt conceded that he was a 'misfit' and that he was not sure why he had gotten into politics in the first place.

In 2012, Dutt was back to campaigning for the Congress again, talking about how he felt so much 'at home' with the party for which his father had dedicated his life. While working on his new, villainous avatar for *Agneepath* (2012)—one of his career defining roles—Dutt told *Mumbai Mirror*, 'Politics is totally over for me. I have realized that politics *meri jagah nahi hai* (politics is not my place). I cannot lecture or spin lies.' Regretting his decision to not be loyal to the party of his father's choice, he said: 'My entire family has been with the Congress right from the time of Pandit Jawaharlal Nehru. Congress is in our blood and as a loyalist, I am always there for Congress. Samajwadi Party was a mistake and I regret it.' Giving Amar Singh a clean chit in the fiasco, he added: 'In fact, he discouraged me (from joining the party). You see, he is not just a politician, but also a brother. But then things happened and those three months in politics were a big lesson for me.'

In March 2013, the Supreme Court upheld Dutt's five-year sentence, eighteen months of which he had already spent in jail during the trial. He was given four weeks to surrender before the authorities. Analysts believed that his imprisonment would have a significant impact on the fortunes of Bollywood. Industrywallahs gave statements to support the ruling and some said they would appeal for his release. Amar Singh and Jaya Prada appealed to the governor of Maharashtra to pardon him.

Dutt was put on parole from 21 December 2013. The parole was extended three times till March 2014 after concerns were raised in Mumbai High Court in a proposal by the government of Maharashtra to amend the parole law. Dutt returned to Yerwada prison after his parole ended. He was out again on a two-week parole granted by the Yerwada Central Jail authorities on 24 December. He said (as reported by *Indian Express*), 'I have lost 18 kgs, if I lose any more weight, I will vanish.' Dutt was subsequently incarcerated in Yerwada Central Jail to complete his jail term.

Now that he is finally free, Dutt has been flirting with politics again, making significant appearances at Bharatiya Janata Party (BJP) events and getting tongues wagging. There has also been sudden speculation that he may step into electoral politics again in Uttar Pradesh. But, while he may flirt with a political rally here and a friendly appearance there, it remains to be seen if he will make public his true political affiliations again—now that there are no real, binding compulsions to do so.

7

Jail House Rock

Perhaps no other public figure in post-Independence India has been in and out of prison as many times as Sanjay Dutt, let alone anyone from a high-profile film family.

His days as a prisoner have inspired both myth and a movie, as the new media, which did not really care about his legacy, shone an unrelenting light on his situation. Here was a story of the decade—the opportunity to chronicle the rise and fall of a super-privileged star as it unfolded; his destiny linked to that of the country's most loved city and its people.

Over the days, news streamed in of Sanjay being placed in solitary confinement at the Yerwada Jail. Reports said he would stare at the lone bulb in the 'anda cell' and watch a line of ants: A fact that was dramatized in his biopic.

In various interviews over time, Sanjay has described his days behind bars as an experience that chastened him, flattened out his ego and gave him an idea of who his real friends were. It was a life-altering experience. In the many anecdotes that filtered out of the prison gates, was also perhaps an attempt to humanize him. Make him appear more fragile, vulnerable and emotionally grounded than what he appeared to be. One such story of his incarceration goes back the '90s—to his time in Thane Central Jail:

Dutt sahab, along with his daughters, visited Sanjay at Thane Central Jail on the day of Rakshabandhan in August 1994. In their biography of Sunil Dutt and Nargis, *Mr and Mrs Dutt—Memories of Our Parents,* Namrata and Priya Dutt write, 'Our eyes filled with tears. We tied a Rakhi on his wrist. Sanjay looked sad and said, "I have nothing to give... This is all I have..."' Sanjay proceeded to offer his sisters two-rupee jail coupons, earned through manual labour. 'It was an extremely emotional moment for us. It was the first time we saw dad break down and cry. We looked at each other in a long embrace and wept, unburdening our hearts, before Sanjay was led back to his cell.' Priya has reportedly held on to the coupons as mementos.

After his jail term, Sanjay began to look at his toughest days with a certain objectivity—a maturity even. He was often asked if he had adopted any strategy to adapt to the hostile and unfamiliar environment, to which he would always shrug, and with a studied nonchalance, say that when one had gone through drugs and addiction, and suffered deaths and tragedies in the family amidst a case that had dragged on for twenty-three years, one could not really live by a 'strategy'. 'These things come to you all of a sudden.

It is like living in the jungles and which animal survives, the predator or the prey. The stronger will survive. My dad told me, one day I am going to die to leave you on the road where people would want to kill you. If you can survive and that too being a good human being, then that will make a big difference. These are things that I learned from my father, with time and experience,' he said in an interview to *The Entrepreneur* magazine.

For those who had been following Sanjay Dutt's journey closely, he was evidently in denial about the enormity of the situation from the moment he returned from Mauritius, where he was shooting for a film, when the news of his involvement in the blasts case first emerged. It was not until they put the handcuffs on him that he broke down—a moment that has been captured by Rajkumar Hirani in *Sanju* as well. He put up a brave front, he said to *Stardust* magazine, for the sake of his father.

The film industry was in a dilemma. One half did not want to be associated with a legal case of such complexity and impact. The other, which was part of the Dutt family inner circle, made it evident that 'Sanju Baba' could have done no wrong. According to Sanjay, the few who dared to stand by him were 'Mahesh Bhatt, Vidhu Vinod Chopra, Raju Hirani, my friends.' There were some in the media too who seemed to empathize with the 'wronged' star. Veteran journalist Rajat Sharma, who hosted Sanjay on his popular show *Aap Ki Adalat*, introduced him as someone who has made more terrible mistakes than anyone in public sphere—but is also the only one whom the fans have forgiven, over and over again. Quite inexplicably.

In fact, it was the conviction that his fans—the people outside the media offices and corridors of power—were willing to overlook his failings, that gave Sanjay Dutt the resolve to get back on his feet. He often spoke about how, even when the judiciary ruled against him, it was his fans who were convinced of his innocence. A peculiar situation to be caught in. While the 'trust' of the people helped him 'fight back', said he to *Entrepreneur India*, 'The most difficult part was that in between all this, my father passed away. He was my anchor and suddenly I was left alone and that too when my judgment was being pronounced. I had to be tough to face it and I thank the judiciary for a fair judgment, after which I was taken out of the terror case and convicted for illegal possession of arms.'

The eight weeks before he went into prison were a blur for Dutt—wrapping up his film projects and spending time with his family. He had no time to break down or confront his fears and anxiety. If he was scared, he did not have the luxury to show it.

It is one thing to try and make sense of the turmoil that had taken over his life. Till the moment he was out of prison, he fought it. Fought for his freedom. But once the law took its own course, and his fate was sealed, there was little else but to make peace with the reality. Surrendering himself to the inevitability, he began to make an effort to stay positive and embrace his Hindu spiritual side. He began to read the *Shiv Puran* and *Ganesh Puran, Mahabharata, Ramayana,* and the *Bhagavad Gita.* His days in Yerwada prison were filled with reading about Hinduism and other religions and getting the inmates together to perform stage plays. He even ran a ham radio station there—Radio YCP—where he would play music and discuss topics such as religion and secularism.

St Lawrence had given Dutt his first taste of the rough and tumble of life, outside the bubble that was his life under his mother's loving gaze. If that experience made a man out of a boy, Yerwada Jail nearly broke that man's back, striking at the knees of his ego.

Dutt was confined to an 8×10 ft cell, and wore the white uniform that all inmates did—a far cry from his signature bomber jackets. He was granted a stroll in a 100 sq ft garden in front of his cell. His neighbouring inmates spoke to the media, commenting on how, after the initial struggle with himself, Dutt resigned himself to his fate. Apparently, he knew he would be released early if he behaved well. Given his-profile and the stature of his case, Dutt was in a high security cell—next to the ward that housed prisoners on death row. He was mostly not allowed to interact with other prisoners. He was never allowed to walk alone or have a stray conversation with anyone without the wardens listening in.

One of the few people who was allowed to exchange a few words with him was the prison librarian. 'I would speak to him as often as I was working as the librarian at the prison,' he said to a BBC journalist later. It was through his words that the picture of Dutt as a voracious reader first began to take shape.

Dutt busied himself with other chores, too. After his morning ablutions, he would be given material to weave bags, and would spend a large part of the morning on this task. A princely sum of ₹45 for a hundred bags was his earning. Just before lunch, he would reach out to his fellow inmates on the prison radio. This show soon became popular—not only for Dutt's ability to hold his audience's attention, but also because he spoke about himself and his struggle with reality, and peppered his life experiences with dialogues from his popular films.

Dutt credits his wife Manyata for playing a huge role during those trying times. 'She has been my anchor after Dutt saab [Sunil Dutt]. She gave me a beautiful home and a beautiful family. She is a strong woman and for her to raise two kids (Shahraan and Iqra) while their father is in jail meant a lot. She would come all the way to Pune every month and she knew that I looked forward to it. Once she just fell down during meeting. Later my lawyer told me that she had 103 fever. When I asked her she told that I did not want to make you feel that I would not come and could not come. You cannot become a bitter person just because you had a bad experience. I had left that in my past.'

The first time he went to prison, Sanjay was in denial. Journalist Khaled Mohammed writes of the incident where he had called up Dutt when the latter was in Mauritius. Pankaj Kharbanda was Dutt's secretary at the time. 'He seemed incredulous about this whole thing,' says Mohammed, and when Khaled tried to tell him that that there were talks of him being involved in the arms possession case and a potential arrest, 'both he and Kharbanda laughed it off. He was like—I am Sanjay Dutt and this couldn't possibly happen to me.' Somewhere between then and when he was convicted and sentenced to prison for the second time—and actually went to prison for the long haul—he realized that no one was going to stand by him and he would have to do this on his own. He began reading up on the law, trying to keep himself abreast of what was happening and taking active interest in the way the case was proceeding. He also tried to distance himself from the media, in a manner of speaking. He realized that perhaps being too accessible to people in order to shake off the image he had of being a 'bad boy' awash in women, booze, drugs and the underworld, was not really working in his favour—and he was only growing older.

Sanjay Dutt has, time and again, blamed the politics of the land for his situation—and his naiveté. 'I had no idea how serious TADA was. And I will tell you one thing—no matter what your profession is, read up on the law of the land. It is very important,' he warned his audience at the Algebra session.

Having been at the heart of one of the most controversial legal cases in modern India, Dutt has come a long way since that day at the Mumbai airport when he was whisked away by the police. He travels the country, addressing people about his drug problem, his fight for freedom and battling the political and legal system—and the demons of his mind. He can wax eloquent about the articles in the original panchnama that had miraculously changed in shape and size over the eighteen years of the case. He will also tell you that had he not admitted to have 'possessed' an assault rifle, there was no other physical proof to hang the case on. And that it took six years for the judicial system to dissolve the TADA charges and press the more benign Arms Possession Act. Though media reports have time and again pooh-poohed his story about self-defence, he has not changed his stance. Like everything else in his life, it was perhaps his honesty that has been his biggest strength and his biggest weakness. *Yes, I am Sanjay Dutt, and yes I did have a gun...*

but... Just as he has time and again confessed to have fought drug addiction for nine years. *Even my father was honest enough to admit to all the producers, that my son did drugs.* Perhaps it is this throwing up of the hands, this artlessness in admitting his biggest 'mistakes', that touched a chord with the common man. At least, it did in the pre-social media days, when people were far more willing to forgive an errant son for graver sins than making a stray remark on Twitter.

8

The Bitter Halves

'I can't believe it's been ten years already,' posted an ecstatic Sanjay Dutt on his Instagram account, celebrating his 10th wedding anniversary with Manyata in February 2018. He even used the hashtag #10YearsOfTogetherness to drive home the point. The media went click happy when Sanjay went out to a restaurant with Manyata and his kids Shahraan and Iqra. He looked dapper in a pair of tattered denim jeans, a leather jacket and a protective arm around his family.

'I am very shy with women,' Sanjay has said over and over again in public. 'I am an introvert.' It may seem strange that the gregarious actor, known for his circle of friends, would say so. But those who know him will tell you that behind the affable veneer is a man who has always had complicated, intense relationships with the women in his life. And not just the ones he was romantically involved with.

Psychologists perhaps would attribute it to an Oedipal complex.

Simi Garewal, on her show—where Dutt often made appearances—recounted an incident from the time Nargis was battling cancer. Simi had dropped in to meet Nargis, who had just returned from the US after her treatment. She was on the bed—emaciated, whimpering, fighting for every breath—and Sanjay was cradling her in his arms, kissing her face and whispering soothing words into her ears. 'That image, of you holding her like your baby, has always remained with me,' said Simi to Sanjay. The end of this powerful mother-child bond, at a time when Sanjay was deep into his addiction, damaged him. And Dutt, who took a long time to ease up with his father, knew that with his mother's death, his life would never be the same again.

Dutt's string of high-profile, controversial relationships began with Tina Munim. Their tumultuous relationship lasted between 1978 and 1983. Tina was a Bandra girl from a Gujarati Jain family—the ninth and youngest child of Nandkumar and Meenakshi Munim. She was a beauty pageant winner and glamour aspirant.

When Sanjay and Tina began dating, they were rebellious, giddy-headed twenty-somethings. The Dutt family was concerned about the son's future. And Tina's fiery, electrifying presence was not exactly their idea of a suitable companion for their mercurial son. Dutt sahab didn't want his son to squander away his time, money and energy on any girl at that important stage of his life. Despite their film industry moorings, they were deeply conservative middle-class in their views on life. And like all middle-class parents, they wanted him to 'study' and be his own self first.

But as it always happens, the more Dutt was persuaded not to meet Tina, the more he rose in defiance. They had secret rendezvous at a mutual friend's tailoring shop, sneaked out for movies and parties, exchanged love notes—basically everything that two young people would do in love to hoodwink the disapproving parents. It was widely believed that the romance would have had a fairy-tale ending had it not been for Tina and her unwillingness to win over the families.

Stardust wrote elaborate reports on how, instead of winning the Dutts over to her side, Tina fought back. 'She made all the wrong moves at the wrong time. And the worst thing she did was to accept Dev Anand's offer to get her launched in films with *Des Pardes*,' said one article. 'Tina, who always wanted to be Mrs Sanjay Dutt more than anything else in the world didn't perhaps know that Bollywood's A-list are not comfortable with the idea of their daughter in laws [sic] returning to work before the camera.' But with the industry warming up to her as a hot, single, ambitious actress, she found a new confidence in herself. She knew she was at par with one of the most influential families in Bollywood at that time—the Dutts.

Tina apparently wanted to snub the family and was soon playing up to her heroes. She apparently wanted to prove to them that Sanjay was not the only man around, revealed an old confidante of Tina to *Stardust*. But her strategy misfired. 'Far from being angry, the Dutts were pleased with Tina's efforts. They hoped that now she will leave their son alone. Sanjay was, however, terribly upset. She seemed to be only complicating matters between them. And her various affairs and little escapades were being blown up in the media,' said another juicy report in the magazine, which followed this love affair relentlessly—perhaps with some embellishment.

In his memoir, *Khullam Khulla*, Rishi Kapoor speaks about how Sanjay Dutt was every bit the possessive lover when Kapoor and Tina were the talk of the town:

> Our budding friendship and the string of movies we did together inevitably led to rampant speculation about a secret affair. The media may not have been as powerful back then as it is today, but people made up stories as blithely then too. I was not married at the time and Tina was seeing Sanjay Dutt. One day, Sanju and Gulshan Grover visited Neetu, at her apartment in Pali Hill. The rumours had gotten to him. Gulshan later told me that during the filming of *Rocky* (Gulshan was also in the film), Sanju had come to Neetu's house to pick a fight with me... She diffused what could have turned into a very ugly scene by calmly explaining to Sanju that the rumours were baseless. She told him, 'There's nothing going on between Tina and Chintu [Rishi Kapoor]. They are colleagues and buddies. You have to learn to trust when you're in this industry.' Later, Sanju and I would laugh over the incident. [Sanju] was high the day he came to Neetu's house too. The truth was established when Neetu and I got married and all my heroines attended the wedding.

After *Rocky*—a film for which she had allegedly refused *Love Story* and several other blockbusters—was released, Tina claimed to gossip magazines that her 'role had been chopped and that the Dutts had taken her for a ride'. The cold war between the Dutts and Tina continued for many years and gossip mills worked overtime, reporting how the Dutt family was instrumental in creating a rift between the two. There were even unsubstantiated reports of how the family had treated her 'very badly on one occasion and that Namrata and Priya were openly rude to her'—none of which can be validated. Wading through the muck that was gathering around the Sanjay-Tina affair, it is difficult to arrive at the truth behind what really transpired. Both parties were using their sources in the media to put forth their side of the story. And no one was complaining! After all, it is not every day that such a potboiler of a story plays out in the public domain.

Fresh out of the relationship, Tina decided to concentrate on her career. In fact, rumour has it that during her relationship with Sanjay, she rejected hit movies such as the aforementioned *Love Story* and *Ek Duje Ke Liye*. In the early '80s, filmmakers started approaching Tina again with prestigious projects and she knew that she had to make the most of it.

Among the films offered, there were a few that paired her with megastar Rajesh Khanna. Tina was naturally ecstatic about being Rajesh Khanna's heroine. They worked in films like *Fifty Fifty* and *Sauten*, both of which were blockbusters. Thus started an eventful professional and personal relationship that lasted through eleven films.

Sanjay was devastated when Tina left him for the much older Khanna. But years later, when Tina got married to Anil Ambani, he showed up as a guest for her wedding.

Tina was just the beginning. Call it the good girls–bad boy syndrome, but Sanjay never fell short of female admiration. Even when he had been sent for drug rehabilitation, there were scores of attractive starlets and heroines who were vocal about their eagerness to work with him, right from Padmini Kolhapure and Poonam Dhillon to a host of others. Nari Hira, the feisty owner and publisher of *Stardust* magazine, ran a series of reports talking to Dutt's female co-stars about how much they missed him. One such story went like this: Poonam Dhillon was desperate to know about his whereabouts when he had been whisked away for drug rehab. She felt protective about him. 'He is so sensitive, you would never want to hurt him,' she confessed. Though they were professional acquaintances, she admitted she 'felt very close to him' whenever they were together. She awaited his return, she said, not just to complete their film *Street Singer,* but even to do a lot more films with him. 'I am sure that the industry will give him a second chance. All he has to do is win back their trust,' she gushed.

The whole crop of newcomers at that time—Divya Rana, Amrita Singh, Natasha Sinha, Meenakshi Seshadri, Vijayta Pandit—were waiting for the star to return and reclaim his place in their lives. Vijayta Pandit told *Stardust*: 'Even if I am just a showpiece or a prop in the film, I just want to be in every frame.' Reem Kapadia (the youngest sister of Dimple Kapadia, she was a small-time actress, known for forgettable films like *Haveli* and *Kaash,* who died early of a drug overdose in 1991), for instance, insisted that Sanjay was the best of the lot of new actors. She accused industrywallahs of manipulating his career. 'I have never met him ... After seeing *Rocky*, I wanted to congratulate him in person and rang him a lot of times but never got through.' Reem had gone to see *Rocky* and she spotted a gang of rowdies who were being paid to create a ruckus during the screening. She believed there were jealous people who were trying to pull him down. 'Watch out, he will be number one. He will take over everybody when he comes back.'

Divya Rana said she was willing to 'jump down a rooftop too' if she got a role with him. She allegedly employed his ex-driver, despite knowing his habit of drinking on duty, only because she loved listening to little incidents about Sanjay Dutt's past. Her love for Sanjay Dutt almost cost her life when the driver nearly fell off the steering wheel. 'Luckily I got hold of the steering from the back seat and saved the situation,' she laughingly confessed to *Stardust*. Despite her love for Rishi 'Chintu' Kapoor, Divya made no bones about the fact that she was extremely attracted to Sanjay Dutt. 'Wow, what a looker. I've always found him extremely fascinating. I go weak in my knees every time I see him. I'm sure all girls feel that way.'

Anita Raj, for the longest time, couldn't forget when she had gone to Jaipur for a shoot and there were about eighty to ninety girls from a nearby hostel who attacked her. She said: 'They didn't want to talk to me. They only wanted to know Sanju's whereabouts. They had seen *Zameen Asmaan* and since Sanju was my co-star in the film, they thought I would know where he is. The girls flooded me with questions like where is Sanju, how is he, when is he coming back? We love him.'

'He has no airs at all. If a light man is smoking a *beedi*, he would take it and smoke it. Not only the heroines, but also the spot boys, technicians, cameraman—everybody will tell you how humble he is,' said Tina Munim, who openly discussed his behaviour in studios. 'He will come back and crush them all. He is too good,' she told *Stardust* after his fall from grace.

Actress Sarika, who allegedly played a part in the Tina–Sanjay affair, got her share of bad publicity but did not hesitate to stick her neck out for the star. 'Sanju must make it this time,' she said about his comeback to the same magazine. 'He must never do anything wrong to go back again. Once you flop here, you flop for good. But the producers, directors and costars [sic] all want to give him a second chance and Sanjay should cash in on it. He has looks, talent everything. He shouldn't waste it.'

Clearly, everybody, especially the women in the film industry, were rooting for the troubled star.

1986 was an important year for Sanjay. He made a stunning comeback with Mahesh Bhatt's *Naam*. Things started looking up for him. And he met his first wife, Richa Sharma.

Richa was born and raised in Delhi before her parents moved to New York. She was a teenager when she met Dev Anand and expressed her desire to work with him. A few years later, the prolific filmmaker signed her on his film *Hum Naujawan* (1985), which catapulted Richa to stardom. A stream of projects came her way with the most buzzing actors of the time—Anil Kapoor, Jackie Shroff, Shekhar Suman and Sanjay Dutt. For the world, Sanjay and Richa met each other for the first time on the set of their first film together, during the mahurat shot. The interaction was brief, professional. But gossip magazines were already sniffing around for more. Apparently, Richa was clueless that Sanjay, who had seen her photographs in film magazines, was crushing on her.

Seconds after the mahurat, Sanjay managed to get Richa's number and asked her out on a date. His reputation preceded him, however, and Richa was hesitant at first. But Sanjay's famous persuasive skills with women eventually won over the talented actress.

Those in the know about this love affair commented on the innocence and the intensity of it. Reports began to surface of how Sanju would make excuses to drop in on her film sets during lunch breaks and write romantic notes to her. He even drafted his make-up man, Muhammed, to play cupid at times. But this whole elaborate affair was carried out discreetly. The Sharma family was not supposed to know—otherwise she would have been whisked off to New York again.

Sanjay finally proposed to Richa when she was shooting *Aag Hi Aag* (1987) in Ooty. She did not give him a straight answer and Sanjay kept calling her till she relented. The Sharma family met the future son-in-law in New York and was floored by his charisma. The young couple got married the same year.

It would seem that Sanjay was finally settled in and enjoying being married. His daughter Trishala was born soon after and in every interview given post marriage, he spoke of how Richa was the best thing that had happened to him. This was probably true to some extent. The rudderless life that he had been leading until then, seemed to be over—if only for a while.

The joy did not last long. Somewhere between *Naam* (1986) and *Khalnayak* (1993), his relationship with Richa started souring, and things came to a head when she was diagnosed with cancer and went off to the US for treatment under the protective gaze of her family. This tumultuous phase in Sanjay's personal life was offset by a golden run at the box office—*Hathyar, Saajan, Sadak* and *Khalnayak*.

Richa, meanwhile, filed for divorce and eventually lost her battle with brain tumour. It was a twin blow to Sanjay. Not only had he lost access to his firstborn, Trishala, the broken marriage had taken on different, far more diabolic colours once Richa was detected with brain tumour. It was almost as if Sanjay had wilfully brought this upon his estranged wife. What's worse—during the time Richa was fighting for her life in the US, he was having a roaring affair with the reigning queen of the marquee, Madhuri Dixit. For Richa, who had nothing to hold on to, this revelation was the proverbial last straw that broke her back and perhaps robbed her of the will to fight back against the disease.

Despite their differences—and there are scores of interviews that Richa gave to film magazines at that point, talking about the mental abuse she had been subjected to and her husband's philandering ways—Sanjay claimed he wanted to be by his ailing wife's side and meet his daughter.

In 1992, Dutt went to jail for possession of arms. Though he managed to get out on bail, he was arrested again a year later. It was reported at that time that showbiz would stand to lose ₹50 crore if he went to prison. He had around twelve films in various stages of production. When things were going completely awry for him on the professional front, his personal life was in turmoil as well. Richa's parents had made it amply clear that they didn't want anything to do with him and Mumbai police wasn't letting him leave the country either.

Sanjay realized he was losing ground with his well-wishers and his fans, and he was determined to change the narrative, one interview at a time. To *Stardust* he said: 'Whenever I am allowed to I will visit Richa in New York. She's been through surgery again. I am pained to read some stories which have made me out to be a cad. I would like to bring my baby Trishala home if I am allowed to. I would write to her from prison and she would write back to me, saying that she misses me very much.'

There are photographs showing Sanjay and his father at Richa's funeral. But it was too little, too late. Richa's family had had enough of their son-in-law, who they believed was responsible for their daughter's unhappy end. They could not save their daughter, but they were not willing to give up their claims to their grandchild Trishala.

In 1998, two years after Richa's death, Sanjay wanted his daughter Trishala to return. Richa's parents took him to court instead. The protracted and rather ugly custody battle didn't work out in Sanjay's favour. He reached out to his favourite journalists and thundered: 'Richa's parents played dirty. They filed a case in New York, forbidding me from visiting Trishala. Why did they stop me from visiting my own child? They think that I was going to kidnap her. They have started the war, I am going to finish it. I have asked my lawyer to get me visiting rights. I don't need to undergo DNA test to prove I am Trishala's father.'

So bitter was the relationship between Richa's parents and the Dutts that when Sunil Dutt pleaded with them to be allowed to meet his grandchild, they left him out in the cold. In an interview with Shoma Chaudhury, Sanjay spoke about how his father would wait on the road to catch a glimpse of Trishala. It shook him to the core and he decided to fight for her custody. He did win a brief reprieve and brought Trishala back to India with him. That's when he realized that she was a fish out of water in his world. 'She wanted Pizza Hut, Big Mac, Coke Lite... I realized she missed her life back in America and I decided [to] take her back.'

By this time, the whole world knew about him and Madhuri—or so they thought. Sanjay, despite his dalliances and the alleged coldness to his wife, did not handle Richa's death well and was in depression for months. On the personal front, right through the '90s, he kept walking in and out of relationships while battling jail sentences.

He reportedly had a fling with the supermodel-turned-actor, Lisa Ray. Although Lisa has always denied the involvement, the two of them were often spotted together. After the Lisa–Madhuri phase, came Rhea Pillai, a relationship that lasted between 1993 and 2005.

There were rumours that one of the reasons why Sanjay Dutt wanted to divorce Richa was that he was serious about Madhuri.

In an interview with *Stardust,* he made a strong case for his loyalty towards his ailing wife. 'I have filed for divorce na? I don't know anything about it. All I know is that I am going to the States in sometime to visit my wife and daughter. So how am I marrying Madhuri? All this may be ok for me, but it's doing Madhuri a lot of harm. She is a lovely person from a good family.'

But he also acknowledged that they had 'terrific chemistry' on-screen.

How was the reigning queen of the marquee responding to this 'affair'? There were reports that Madhuri, who was known to be reserved, had transformed radically after meeting Sanjay. She was more accessible and looked happy. She seemed to have found joy beyond the camera and lights.

It's interesting that Madhuri, who has worked with everyone—Aamir Khan, Jackie Shroff, Vinod Khanna—over the years, would share such crackling chemistry with Sanjay. On the face of it, the two had very little in common. Madhuri came from a very middle-class suburban Mumbai family. She had no sense of entitlement or privileges and had worked her way up the stardom ladder. And then happened *Thanedaar*, and suddenly she seemed to have a lot to share with her controversial co-star. The initial days of exchanging pleasantries soon gave way to more substantial interactions, and their bond grew stronger. Sanjay may not have had a clue about where she was coming from, but certainly knew where she was and where she wanted to be. Negotiating stardom and the loneliness that came with it, and dealing with a fragile heart—these shared life experiences brought the two top stars closer.

A standard practice in film journalism—of the Indian kind—is to ascribe controversial quotes to 'friends of stars' and 'sources.' Especially when the stars wish for certain information to be circulated in the media but wish to distance themselves from it. The practice serves well to couch speculation and hearsay in a veil of authenticity. In the alleged Sanjay–Madhuri love affair, reports emerged of how the two stars were gushing about each other to their 'close friends'. Labels and adjectives flew thick and fast: 'affectionate and caring man' and 'gorgeous and wonderful human being' among them.

When they were both in Bombay or shooting together, the stars would meet. But when one of them had to go out of station for a location shoot, the long phone calls began. While shooting for *Sadak* in Ooty, Sanjay spoke to Madhuri every day. The unit members witnessed these long-distance calls that went on for hours. This was way before the first mobile phone reached India. When they were shooting in two different continents—Sanjay in London, shooting for J.P. Dutta's *Kshatriya* and Madhuri in Nairobi, shooting for Rakesh Roshan's *Khel*—they embarked on long international calls.

The intense relationship was beginning to show in Madhuri's career choices. Despite her successful pairing with Aamir Khan in *Dil,* Madhuri seemed disinterested in leveraging it. She chose another film with Sanjay instead and the two of them signed a number of films together—*Saajan, Saahibaan, Mahaanta.* Being cast together would mean they would get to see more of each other. The whole industry was abuzz.

Not enough is known about what really went wrong in this relationship between the two reigning stars of the time, even though certain things were obvious. In Sanjay's own words, 'There was a certain magic in *Saajan, Sahibaan* and *Khalnayak. Mahaanta,* our last film together was a disaster because halfway through, MD (Madhuri Dixit) and I stopped talking. Naturally, the film was completed under stress.'

Madhuri, after she moved on, resurrected her career, got married to US-based doctor Shriram Nene and moved to the US, has always refused to talk about her relationship with Sanjay. But why was Madhuri so averse to talking about the relationship that was playing itself out in public?

This denial first came to light when Dutt was in prison for the first time. Tremors were felt in the film industry when Madhuri reportedly severed her ties during this time. The public outrage over what many regarded as an injustice to Sanjay was enormous, but what upset people even more was Madhuri's inexplicable behaviour—the perception that she had turned her back on her alleged lover. After months of a roaring affair, she did not visit Sanjay in jail even once, or attempt to contact him. For all intent and purposes, Madhuri just didn't seem to care about what happened to her Sanjay one way or the other. This, from someone who was believed to be keen to get married to him. Her refusal to stand by the man who had, till then, had such a strong presence in her life, did not cast her in a favourable light. But one must consider that traditionally, Hindi film heroines have much shorter shelf lives than the men. They are judged more often and their careers are much more vulnerable to gossip and accidents. Madhuri knew at the time that she had barely a few years to go to make the most of her influence and success at the box office. And she could, in no way, swap that with being dragged indirectly into a case that involved terror links, arms and a man whose reputation was scarred forever. It is one thing to romance a guy who has had stints with drugs and a troubled childhood, but was always an A-list actor. It is quite a different story to be linked with a man who has had established terror links and went to prison because of it.

Rumours, especially the swirling tabloid reports, say that when Sanjay attempted to talk to Madhuri over the phone while he was in jail, she allegedly banged the phone down the minute she heard his voice.

But there is more to this break up than the shadow of the underworld.

According to 'sources' again, the story behind the breakup of the glamorous couple went back a couple of months or more, before the date of Sanjay's arrest.

It was in Ooty, during the shooting of Sajid Nadiadwala's *Andolan*, where Sanjay's co-star was Somy Ali, who allegedly had a crush on him. Somy was also reportedly having an affair with Salman Khan at that time, and it was unlikely that she would rekindle her romantic interest in Sanjay, who was obviously seeing Madhuri. But something happened. And the two stars, far away from prying eyes, in the salubrious environment of the picturesque hill station, reportedly got close. Things would have remained on the sets, had it not been for Madhuri's decision to surprise her love by turning up on location. Reports sprang up from the set of the film of how Madhuri walked in on the two of them in a compromising position, and walked out—but not before giving them a piece of her mind.

She did not care to walk back into Sanjay's life again.

Nevertheless, Madhuri's denial of this relationship has been so strong that there were rumours that she had called up the makers of *Sanju* and asked to not be mentioned in the biopic. Recently, however, when Madhuri was addressing the media during a press conference for a Marathi film, she clarified these allegations. 'This is complete rubbish. I never called Raju, neither did we speak about the film that you are talking about. Moreover, I have moved on, and I would suggest everyone should move on too.' In fact, Madhuri's long-time manager Rikku Rakeshnath mentioned to *Stardust,* 'It was a deliberate move by the producer and director to spread false stories of romance around my client Madhuri and Sanjay Dutt to create hype in the media before the release of the movie. Both knew that it was false news, but kept quiet because it was working professionally in their favour.'

The two actors would eventually work together again in *Kalank* (2019), putting to rest the speculations about their continued awkwardness.

★

After Richa's death, losing his child's custody, becoming infamous for his alleged underworld and terror links and being dumped by Madhuri, Sanjay met Rhea Pillai, who was an Art of Living practitioner, a model and a socialite. Though they seemed to have very little in common, Rhea started giving him the kind of emotional strength and stability that he always craved for in a relationship. It is said that Sanjay always managed to arouse maternal instincts in the women that he dated and married, and Rhea Pillai was probably no exception.

In 1995, he moved in with Rhea. She seemed to be a calming influence on him, because he seemed to be getting his life back on track. He was out on bail, thanks to his father, and with his movie *Vaastav*, he reestablished himself as someone who could actually be an actor as well. Sanjay spoke of the new woman in his life with characteristic deference: 'We will tie the knot sometime this year. Marriage or no marriage, Rhea will always be a part of me. The wedding ceremony will just be a formality.' When he was first imprisoned for thirteen months, Rhea was seen making innumerable trips to the jail. As soon as he was out, Sanjay married her in 1998.

The new millennium turned things around for Sanjay. Even though his relationship with Rhea did not work out (yet again) for various reasons, 2000 was the biggest turning point in Sanjay Dutt's career—thanks to Rajkumar Hirani and the Munna Bhai midas touch. Almost overnight, Sanjay went from 'khalnayak' to 'nayak'. He became a hero of the masses because of the role that he played and the conviction with which he played it. It seemed that Indian audiences were willing to overlook all the wrongs in his life—because they loved the character so much. A fine example of how reel and real often overlap.

Munna Bhai worked, but the marriage didn't. He and Rhea were divorced and Sunil Dutt passed away around this time. Sanjay began to look for company, for solace. Many believe that Rhea left Dutt because he was openly involved with Nadia Durrani during the filming of *Kaante* in 2002. Twenty-seven-year-old Nadia was a divorcee with a nine-year-old daughter. But Sanjay was reportedly smitten by her. In fact, after Sanjay returned to India following filming for *Kaante* in the US, they were in touch and finally appeared on the scene in 2007 when he introduced her as his girlfriend to his close friends. Despite strong rumours about the two of them getting married, Nadia exited his life as quickly as she had come in.

Lonely, embattled and beleaguered, Sanjay was looking for another emotional anchor when he met Manyata. The coming of Manyata in his life would prove to be a very, very significant moment in his personal graph, especially because of the way he got married to her. Manyata was not exactly the kind of person that the Dutt family—Namrata and Priya—would ever approve of. There was an age difference of twenty years between the two. She wasn't considered classy, educated or good-looking enough to be Sanjay Dutt's wife and he surprised everyone, including his family, when he just called them up and said he was getting married.

Sanjay put his wife on a public pedestal, according her the kind of respectability and status that would silence his detractors—for a while, at least. He spoke of how his wife was a grounded girl who reminded him of his mother. A simple, domestic person, who made it worth the while to come home after living like a gypsy.

Manyata was everything that his previous women were not. She was also everything he seemed to want at that stage in his life. She compensated for her lack of pedigree, finesse or glamour, by being someone who was completely devoted to him and put his well-being over everything else—even if it cost him his old friendships and closest relationships.

His sisters did not attend the wedding. It was just the beginning.

9

The 'Final' Mrs Dutt

After a two-year courtship, Sanjay Dutt and Manyata made things official by tying the knot at the Taj Exotica in Goa on 7 February 2008, in accordance with Hindu rituals.

Until that time, the world knew very little about this mystery woman who was twenty years his junior. In a chat show with internationally acclaimed designers Abu Jani and Sandeep Khosla, Manyata articulated what many would have felt at that time: 'No one probably imagined that I will be the "final" Mrs Dutt.'

Manyata was neither Bollywood aristocracy, nor was her past something she would talk about—two instant disqualifiers in a star union. Right from the word 'go', it was obvious that she did not have too many friends in the film fraternity. In sync with the wedding news, videos emerged of her doing an item number in Prakash Jha's

sexist 'investigations.' The age gap was not something people were willing to overlook, nor were they okay with the stark contrast in their social statures. Despite Sanjay's tryst with legal cases, the stain of terror, his image of a heartbreaker and homewrecker, his drug addiction, and a hundred other vices, he was still the Dutt family scion. That surname alone, and his exalted status in the industry, absolved him of all his sins in a patriarchal system. Manyata had no such luck. She tried to fit in by loving every bit of her husband's universe—the good, the bad and the ugly.

Given her belief that fair-weather friends were taking advantage of Sanjay's 'good nature', there were things she wanted to 'fix'. In the Abu-Sandeep chat show, she confessed, 'If I hadn't taken charge of Sanju's money, he would have spent all of it in buying cars and watches and giving loans to his loser friends!'

She was the wife who cracked the whip and took care of the messy bits in the husband's life. And it didn't go down well with a large number of people. Sanjay, on the other hand, simply seemed thankful that there was finally someone in his life who was keeping him stable.

Before she became a mother, Manyata used to run a textile business, for which she had to keep long hours. Sanjay wanted her to quit. She eventually did, and shifted her focus completely to being producer for the home banner. In her own words, 'I've never been ambitious about being an actress or a star in that sense'—perhaps because she was only focused on being Mrs Sanjay Dutt? Not everybody wants to be in that kind of a spotlight. Some people are perfectly happy sharing it with their partners. As she jokingly replied in the Abu-Sandeep chat show when they asked her what it was like to be Mrs Dutt, 'Getting invited to a show like this!'

There were other issues, besides family and naysayers, which would really test the relationship. For instance, she was twenty-nine and Dutt was forty-nine, which did not make it easy for them to start a family. Manyata later revealed that she had a couple of miscarriages, after which they went for in vitro fertilization (IVF)—leading to the birth of their twins, Shahraan and Iqra. Things truly started changing for the family at that time. Perhaps the toughest challenge Manyata had to face as Sanjay Dutt's wife—which underscores her importance in his life—was when he had to go back to prison. This was tougher than winning over Trishala, the sisters, or his friends who now felt alienated.

Manyata spoke of the episode as something that shattered her completely. For her, five further years of jail to top off fifteen years of having to live with the case was far too harsh on Sanjay. She tried desperately to buy time for him before he went back to prison. She would fly down to Delhi and confer with the lawyers every day (something that has been dramatized in the film to great effect), come back late at night and manage to catch some sleep only on the flight. Despite her complete exhaustion, she continued to fight for her husband, who was rushing to finish his projects before he went back to prison and was in no shape to focus on anything else. He was at his second professional peak, and crores of rupees were riding on him. Manyata pulled out all the stops and they managed to buy a month's time.

She recounts a moment when, amidst the drama, heartbreak

and anxiety of Sanjay being taken back to prison, fans had gathered outside the jail to shout and chant his name. He stood in front of them with folded hands and said, 'Let me surrender.'

The moment Sanjay went back to prison, everyone who had invested money in him, not least the producers, wanted it back. They were ready to write him off; as he would probably be far too old once he came out of prison. He would be finished. Sanjay, himself, was in depression. He too was convinced that his career was over. Manyata was the one who tried to ensure that things were up and about and running smoothly. She struggled to make ends meet and pay off producers. Property they owned in Mumbai had been leased out to the American Consulate, but they refused to be associated with it following Sanjay's arrest, backing out of the lease. Somehow, she managed—and even began working on her home production banner. She also had to hold the fort at home, and pretend to the children that their father was away on work. It helped that they were used to long absences on his part owing to shoots.

Unsurprisingly, Manyata's health started failing. She was diagnosed with a congenital heart condition. There was also a tumor in her liver. She had collapsed during one of her trips to Singapore, in the aftermath of which they discovered several complications. She had to undergo surgery. She also started losing clumps of her hair, leading to speculation that she had cancer and was undergoing chemotherapy. With all the odds stacked heavily against her, Manyata retreated into a shell. It was only thanks to the likes of producer Krishika Lulla, that she agreed to step out in public.

The outing was ill-timed. There was uproar when Sanjay wished to meet her on parole. She had been spotted at the premiere of Krishika Lulla's film *Rambo Rajkumar*, and the general perception was that there was nothing really wrong with her. The parole was initially refused on the grounds that there weren't enough medical documents to support her condition, apart from a certificate from Saifi Hospital. It was at this moment that Priya Dutt, who had been antagonistic towards Manyata until then, stepped in. Empathy came in the form of Shah Rukh Khan as well, who visited her at her home and encouraged her to cut her hair short (and stylish) to deal with the hair loss.

The couple's relationship hit a tender patch at this time. Sanjay would write to Manyata regularly from prison, and they would have long conversations in Hindi over letters. Her relationship with Trishala also improved over time, and they hung out together in New York. The reason Trishala never visited Dutt in prison was because the family wanted it this way. They didn't want any of the three children to be here—especially Trishala. They didn't want her to come to Mumbai and be hounded by the media. Perhaps that was a wise decision after all.

It was Manyata who gave Rajkumar Hirani the idea of making *Sanju*. Hirani, another staunch friend who stood by the family through these trying times, had scripts for *Munna Bhai 3* lying around, which could not be produced until Sanjay was out of jail. Manyata suggested that he make a film on her husband instead, and proceeded to narrate some incidents from his life. Over the course of filming, Ranbir Kapoor would check on her regularly. Arjun Kapoor was the other actor who was generous with his help during some tough times, Manyata has revealed.

A change in perception had happened and not everyone was sitting in judgement of the woman who was the 'final Mrs Dutt.' Everyone knew that she had her hands full fighting her own ill health, keeping the children insulated from the controversy and helping Sanjay preserve his sanity. Today, Manyata, who is grateful for all the help, feels that she is in a much stronger position.

There is no denying the fact that she has been the most important chapter in Sanjay's life. At every possible juncture, at every interview, at every gathering, he has only spoken of his wife with the highest respect. And that was a sign that the proverbial bad boy was actually mellowing, maturing—becoming more human in some ways. His image of being a little boy trapped in an adult's body, which explained his rash, irrational, impulsive decisions for a lot of people, also made them all too eager to write off his marriage to Manyata. There is no way this is going to last, they would say. But something truly had changed since the Rhea Pillai days. Not only did the marriage survive, it soldiered through some truly trying times.

In the same interview with IANS, talking about her dating days with Sanjay and how things changed after marriage, Manyata happily said: 'Oh yes. I've never been happier. Sanju has stood by me through thick and thin. I've known him for nine years. We started seeing each other seriously in 2005. But he knew my past. So when "friends" tried to provoke him he just laughed it off. He knew everything about me. When I was going through hell before my marriage, I'd pick up the phone and ask him for help. We're both very positive people and we like to live and let live. We both believe in forgiving. And we believe every saint can have a past. And every sinner can have a future.'

Namrata, in fact, spoke about her reaction to Sanjay marrying Manyata. 'A night before he was getting married, I got a message from him saying that I am getting married tomorrow. We didn't attend the ceremony because somewhere we felt left out. But things changed again when Manyata gave birth to twins Shahraan and Iqra, and the family was together again. All of us made an effort to work things out when Manyata got pregnant. My equation with her is good, says Namrata. She calls me didi, she is pretty well adjusted to Sanjay, his life and the children. She has made many changes to fit into his lifestyle. They are happy.'

Two months after the commencement of Sanjay's sentence was Manyata's birthday, which she chose not to celebrate. Sanjay, for this special occasion, plucked a red rose from the jail's garden and kept it in between the pages of a book, on which he wrote a poem for Manyata. It reportedly made this stoic, headstrong woman tear up.

10

Friends and Foes

If a man is known by the company he keeps, Sanjay Dutt would appear to be a man who thought with his heart and rarely used his head.

A large part of Sanjay's charisma was thanks to his man-boy appeal: the bulk of a brontosaurus with the emotional quotient of a seven-year-old. A man who is always a boy with the boys, would never be short of colourful company. Neither would he be wanting in fiercely loyal friends. And that's how it happened for this star, who grew old without really growing up.

As a teenager—or even later—Sanjay always had a crowd of friends around him—the boys' club. His mother and his aunt Zaheeda were convinced, and not without reasons, that this bunch was responsible for his drug addiction and other vices. They believed their son was largely blameless and that he took to drugs after boarding school as a recreational habit. In fact, in the interview with Shoma Chaudhury, Sanjay claimed that even while he was in Sanawar, he eventually formed a close group of friends, with whom he would smoke the occasional marijuana and drink country liquor.

Back in the city, when he was in college, Sanjay claims he was extremely tongue-tied in the presence of women. At a party, he recounts, a friend offered him coke. And thus began a long and tumultuous relationship with drugs. As word got around of his addiction, there were more 'friends' who plied him with more recreational drugs until he moved on to heroine. In the Simi Garewal interview, he spoke of how he had turned into a 'rat', locked up in his room and bathroom all the time. His family, says Dutt sahab had no experience of dealing with a drug addict, and for the most part, was in denial. Until, of course, that day he woke up after a forty-eight-hour heroine stupor and all hell broke loose. The friends from his drug days did not quite give up on him. Sanjay recounts that after he returned from his US rehab, he wanted to keep a low profile. As soon as he got home, someone pressed the doorbell. It was his dealer and a former friend. 'When no one, other than my family, knew about my return, this guy not only found out that I was back, but he had assumed that I will want to do drugs again,' said Sanjay. The 'friend' stood there with a pack of a new drug. Dutt thought for a second. There was nothing to stop him from going back—but he had everything to lose if he did. He kicked the guy out—a moment that has been immortalized in his biopic.

But there were other friendships that he nurtured, with reciprocation.

In 2016, right after Sanjay walked out of prison, free at last, there was a party at his buddy and brother-in-law Kumar Gaurav's new pad. Besides close family, there were a handful of his friends who had been invited. One of them even sat on his lap, as the two 'boys' re-lived their boisterous days as chaddi buddies.

Paresh Ghelani has been a constant at some of Sanjay's most special parties over three decades. The Chicago-based entrepreneur even flew down to Tanzania in 2017 to celebrate with his bestie, who turned fifty-eight that year. Sanjay calls him 'Parya', and even took him along to meet Narendra Modi when he was the chief minister of Gujarat in 2010—and not just for small talk. Ghelani, a Gujarati from Ahmedabad who migrated to the US, has diverse interests—and a Hollywood-style film studio and theme park in Gujarat was on his agenda at the time. While one does not know how serious he was about his 'dream project', Parya has always been dead serious about being with his friend. That this has been a special bond is evident from the fact that Vicky Kaushal, the actor playing his friend in *Sanju,* had been flown down to meet Parya just to get the nuances right.

Sanjay has often claimed that there are three or four men whom he considers to be his best friends. Other than Parya, there is a certain Mac from Los Angeles, who he befriended during his rehab stint, Imran Ismail, and, of course, Kumar Gaurav.

Kumar Gaurav, who eventually married Sanjay's sister, Namrata, is veteran actor Rajendra Kumar's son. It is said when Sanjay was going through one of his first lean phases after *Rocky* for five years—when he was struggling, had no films and was in deep trouble;

Kumar Gaurav picked up the film that revived his career.

Mahesh Bhatt had discussed the basic idea of the film that was to become *Naam*—a tale of two brothers—with Kumar Gaurav, who thought it was a great idea and wanted to produce it under his father's production banner. Rajendra Kumar being a veteran of the industry, realized at once that it was a bad idea as far as his son was concerned—he knew that the audience would empathize more with the darker, more complex character. Especially when that character was to be played by Sanjay Dutt. But Kumar Gaurav insisted that they produce the film.

Interestingly, this film was also important for Salim Khan, who had split from his writing partner Javed Akhtar and was not really getting any significant work because most people thought Javed was the real writer in the jodi. Bhatt approached Salim to write the script. This unusual story about two half-brothers sprung to life with Salim Khan's touch. Interestingly, Salim later wrote the dialogues for *Vaastav*, which would be another important milestone in Sanjay Dutt's career.

Kumar Gaurav turned out to be a messiah for his buddy with *Naam*. Despite family problems, the two have always rallied around each other during times of crisis.

When Dutt came out of prison for the first time, he decided to live on his own—and it was Kumar Gaurav who stood by him. In several interviews, Kumar Gaurav has repeatedly spoken of how his friendship with his former buddy is not exactly the way it used to be, even though Gaurav and Namrata's children were really close to Sanjay. When they went to meet him in the jail for the first time,

At the mahurat of Jung *(2000), with Aditya Pancholi and Jackie Shroff*

On set

On the set of Jodi No. 1 *(2001), with Govinda and Praveen Shah*

At the music release of Khoobsurat *(1999), with Subhash Ghai*

On the set of Vaastav *(1999), with director Mahesh Manjrekar*

Rhea Pillai

With Smita Thackeray

On the set of Vaastav *(1999), with director Mahesh Manjrekar*

Rhea Pillai

With Smita Thackeray

On the set of Vaastav *(1999), with director Mahesh Manjrekar*

Rhea Pillai

With Amitabh Bachchan

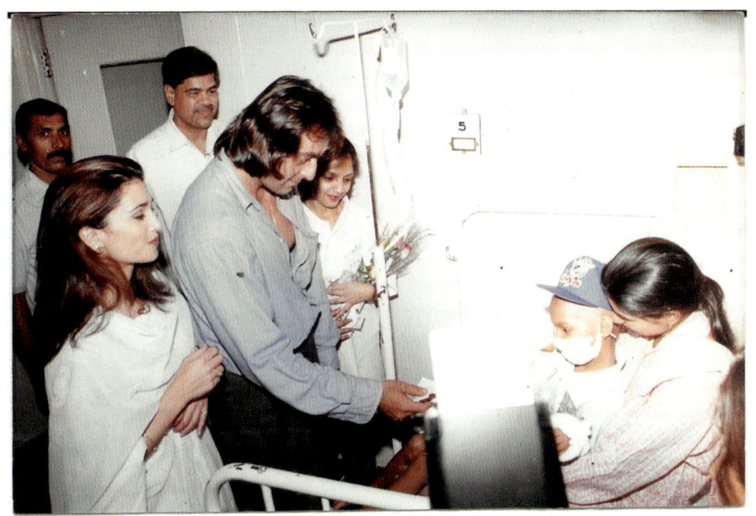

With Rhea Pillai, visiting cancer patients

Sanjay Dutt, Bollywood's bodybuilding pioneer

With Akshaye Khanna

With Anil Kapoor

With director Raj Kanwar on the set of Daag: The Fire *(1999)*

With Mahesh Bhatt

With Madhuri Dixit

With Madhuri Dixit, Subhash Ghai and Jackie Shroff (left to right)

With Mahesh Manjrekar

With Manisha Koirala in Khauff *(2000)*

With Mohd. Azharuddin and Sangeeta Bijlani

With Pooja Bhatt

With Priyanka Chopra

With Rhea Pillai

With Shatrughan Sinha

With Smita Thackeray

Father and son

In Kaante *(2002)*

the children broke down and had a lot of trouble coming to terms with the fact that their beloved Mamu was behind bars; perhaps this was a reason why they distanced themselves from each other.

While some of his oldest friendships have withstood the test of time, the ones forged later seem to have had their share of ups and downs. And the one friendship that has mirrored his own chequered life is the one he shared with his Gups—Sanjay Gupta.

With Gups, Sanjay shared more than just his first name. They loved the same things in life: guns, gizmos, living on the edge—and films, where all of these came together. Sanjay Dutt met Gupta during the shooting of *Street Singer*. The film never got made, but the boys struck a rapport. When Gupta sought to make a directorial debut, he had the Sippys produce his signature mishmash of a script—a bit of *Deewar*, a bit of Jon Woo's *A Better Tomorrow* and background scores and scenes that had been inspired by countless other films. *Aatish*, when it released in 1994, was a talking point for more than one reason. While rumours suggested Salman Khan had been replaced by Sanjay for the lead, Amitabh Bachchan flagged off the muhurat shot, making his affection for Dutt Junior official. But the film, that had Sanjay create a stir with his freshly crafted beefiness, also marked the beginning of Gupta's brand of slick, stylish and highly unoriginal films—and his mentor's twenty-three-year-old legal battle. It was during the Mauritius schedule of this film that news broke of Dutt's involvement with the 1993 Bombay Blast case.

While Aatish released to a reasonably successful box office response, these two namesakes were soon to be the industry's best known blood brothers. Gupta created some of the most exciting projects for Dutt—*Khauff, Kaante, Musafir* and *Dus Kahaniyaan.* Not all these films were successful, but it created 'brand Gupta' and cemented Sanjay Dutt's position as a de facto reel gangster who is at ease everywhere from Shanghai to Saki Naka.

Sanjay Dutt has often acknowledged that it was because of the inspiration and encouragement that he received from Gupta's films that he could actually take the plunge in making a film together. The two inseparables started a production house called White Feather Films. The idea was to keep making more films about the only things they were fascinated with—the underworld, guns, bikes and big boys in bomber jackets.

It would have been a dream run for Messrs Sanjay and Sanjay—had it not been for a certain gent, Dharam Oberoi, who spoiled the party. *Shootout at Lokhandwala,* one of their most high-profile joint ventures, tested their friendship. There were rumours that Gupta was mishandling the budgets for *Shootout at Lokhandwala,* and Sanjay Dutt was unhappy at the way things were being done. Though Gupta later said that one of the biggest problems with Sanjay Dutt was that he could be easily misled, something just snapped between the two former best friends and they parted ways bitterly. Tongues wagged, reams were written and speculation was rife about what could really have caused the rift between the best buddies. Though sources from the Dutt camp claimed that he felt he was being exploited, Gupta later blamed Dharam Oberoi, Dutt's manager, for the misunderstanding. In an interview with *Bombay Times,* Gupta said that his friend was 'kaan ka kaccha' (prone to believing hearsay)—something Dutt would accuse author Yasser Usman of, many years later.

But this was no ordinary fallout. The two were bound by a far more sinister thread beyond their love for slick action films—their fascination with the underworld and an ill-advised urge to play with fire. In 2002, the media received and promptly published transcripts of the conversation that Sanjay Dutt had had with the dreaded underworld don Chhota Shakeel. And he was not alone. With him were Gups, filmmaker Mahesh Manjrekar (who made *Vaastav* with him) and producer Harish Sugandh. The tapes proved the depth of the nexus between Bollywood's top stars and filmmakers, and the mafia.

Among other publications, *Outlook India* ran the entire transcript of Dutt's conversation with the don in 2000. It was evident that Sunil Dutt's son was perfectly at ease talking to India's most wanted criminal—Dawood Ibrahim's lieutenant. In the tapes, Dutt is 'heard' seeking favours for his friend and even discussing the bee in his bonnet—his frenemy—the other notorious gangster, Abu Salem. In all this, Gupta sounds complicit.

In his book, *My Name Is Abu Salem,* senior crime journalist and bestselling author Hussain Zaidi writes about how Gupta and Dutt were on the run after their attempts to play one don against the other backfired:

> Sanjay and Salem were of course good friends once upon a time—Salem in complete awe of Sanjay and the star enjoying the attention. The running joke in the Mumbai underworld

had been that Salem did not bathe for three days after having delivered the AK-56 to Sanjay Dutt before the riots...

A telephone conversation recorded on 14 July 2002, exposed Sanjay Dutt's connections with Shakeel. The transcripts would later be produced in the MCOCA (Maharashtra Control of Organised Crime Act) court where Sanjay would have to explain them away by saying he was too drunk and didn't have the slightest clue who he was talking to.

Salem had by then fallen out with his former boss Anis Ibrahim and was aware that he and Shakeel were stalking him at every turn. What he did not know was that they had also allegedly involved his one-time friend Sanjay Dutt in a plot to eliminate him in New Jersey.

For the record, the actor has always denied his involvement in such a conspiracy.

According to unconfirmed reports, Salem had told his old friend Sanjay that he would attend one of the star-studded live Bollywood shows in New Jersey.

Salem wanted to drop by and say hello to Sanjay and his other 'friends' in Bollywood. After all, this was 2001 and he was living inconspicuously in the US. Not many in Bollywood knew that Salem was trying to settle down in Chicago and was making efforts to extend his base to Los Angeles and New Jersey.

Salem had confided only in Sanjay about his plans to attend the event. Maybe he wanted to make it seem like a casual visit to a 'Bollywood night' while he was on a trip to the

US, and wanted to give away nothing about his whereabouts in the country.

At the very last minute, however, the gangster received some chilling intelligence and cancelled his visit to the event.

Chhota Shakeel had hatched a plot to kill Salem in New Jersey, he was told. Shakeel's gunmen had conducted a recce of the stadium and were planning to strike as soon as Salem appeared at the glittering event.

Salem had heard that it was Sanjay who had tipped Shakeel off about his expected presence at the event. Salem was only too well aware of Shakeel's skills and resourcefulness and how well he could plan an attack.

Only a few months ago, on September 15, 2000, Shakeel had orchestrated an audacious attack on Chhota Rajan in his den in Bangkok. Rajan had survived by the skin of his teeth.

Salem decided to cancel his visit to New Jersey, but harboured a massive grudge against Sanjay and had decided to punish him for his treachery and betrayal.

A few months later, Salem organised four gunmen to 'take care of' Sanjay.

The actor was in Goa at the time, along with his friend and the director of *Kaante*, Sanjay Gupta, known to him as Gups. Salem's instructions to his boys were clear: Go after Sanjay and kill him in Goa or at Mumbai airport upon his return.

But Sanjay and Gups heard of the planned hit and desperately began working the phones to get help. They asked several friends of Salem's to mediate, but these men found

Salem in no mood to forgive Sanjay Dutt.

Sanjay and Gups remained holed up in the hotel room until they managed to get hold of a close friend of Salem's in Mumbai by the name of Akbar Khan. This man had helped Salem in the days when the don was on the run from the Mumbai police after the serial blasts.

Khan had helped Salem cross the border and had even driven him to Kathmandu in his own car. It was a huge risk for him to take and Salem was so grateful to Khan that he never refused him a thing.

When Gups asked Khan to intervene, the latter agreed. After all, who would not want to oblige a successful and affluent filmmaker?

Khan called up Salem and asked him to rein in his shooters.

Salem was furious, but also couldn't say no to Khan. He told him that his hitmen would not touch the two Sanjays so long as they travelled in Khan's car.

The news of amnesty was conveyed to the beleaguered actor-director duo, much to their immense relief. They managed to reach Mumbai airport and Khan ferried them across town in his Hyundai Santro, saving them from the wrath of Salem and his shooters.

Khan was no Good Samaritan. Over the next few months, he regularly visited Sanjay Gupta's plush office in Lokhandwala and took lakhs of rupees for something or the other, part of the unwritten price for his help.

Gupta resented it, but shelled out the money quietly. He could hardly irk Khan and invite bad luck home.

While Khan extracted hard cash from Gupta, he ensured that Sanjay Dutt, whose market price at the time was a couple of crores per film, worked in his own movie for free.

Market analysts dubbed the movie as the most disastrous of Sanjay's career and wondered what made him take up the movie just as his career was peaking.

Salem later boasted that he decided to forgive Sanjay because the actor had called him on his satellite phone (which used to cost Rs 1,000 per minute for a call) and tearfully sought his forgiveness.

Salem would boast about this incident, saying to his audience that he had decided to forget Sanjay's betrayal out of the goodness of his heart.

*

When you defy death threats and go to hell and back together, you would imagine that your friendship would survive the odds. But in this case, Sanjay chose to exit, even though Gupta clung on to the memories of the giddy days of their bonhomie.

This 'blood' bond coming to an end took an emotional toll on Gupta and he couldn't commit himself to directing a film for a long time after his last one with Dutt.

In an interview with *Filmfare* in 2013, when Sanjay Dutt had to go to prison again after the Supreme Court sentencing, Gupta claimed there was no bad blood between him and his former bestie anymore. 'We've been talking to each other and I even have a script for him. Imagine if his and Bachchan Saab's characters had not died in *Kaante,* I want to bring together again a gang of middle-aged gangsters, talking about past exploits and gearing towards one last hit. I wonder if I can make that film now.' Talking about why they fell apart in the first place, he said, 'I believed he'd have more faith in me than in shady people like Dharam Oberoi. I wonder why he didn't trust our friendship of twenty years. I wonder why he let himself be surrounded by people who spoilt his relationships. I was hurt and kept waiting for his call. He must have waited for mine. People took advantage of our lack of communication.'

While addressing media for his film *Kaabil,* Gupta made a rather controversial statement on Sanjay Dutt's biopic. 'I don't want it made, then why would I direct it?' He had apparently spoken to Dutt about a book trilogy on his life instead. 'Phase one would feature his life as a child of superstar parents, addiction and rehab. Phase two would have him returning and becoming a star, ending with the guns episode. And the last part would be the eventual court case and his life today. It'd make the most fascinating read. There is only so much you can show in a two-hour movie as against a book that can capture so much more,' he concluded during the press conference.

★

Rumours had suggested for a while that it was Manyata who was beginning to call the shots in Sanjay Dutt's life, but after she was put in charge of his production house, she allegedly began to edit his friend list and professional list as well. Nonetheless, Dutt and Gupta did patch up—they have been socializing, they exchanged calls; they are on good terms once again. But according to Gupta, that spark is no longer there and they haven't worked together again yet.

As far as Dharam Oberoi is concerned, he has been an important catalyst in Sanjay Dutt's life—and not all of it for the better. Oberoi replaced Pankaj Kharbanda, who had been a friend, confidante and mentor for Dutt besides being his business manager-cum-secretary-cum-father figure. In fact, when Sanjay returned to his shocking welcome at Mumbai airport from Mauritius, it was Kharbanda who had held the fort. As Kharbanda's replacement, Oberoi's alleged high-handedness cost Sanjay a number of friendships. Sanjay Gupta was one of the casualties during his tenure as a secretary-cum-manager for Dutt. The other one was the film that he did with Ram Gopal Varma (RGV).

Department was directed by RGV and starred Sanjay Dutt, Amitabh Bachchan, and Rana Daggubati in the lead roles, alongside Anjana Sukhani and Abhimanyu Singh in pivotal roles. The film released on 18 May 2012, and was universally panned by critics. It was made on a budget of ₹30 crore and it made just about ₹7 crore. True to his style, RGV lashed out on Twitter, attacking Dutt and Dharam Oberoi and asserting that he would never work with them again. They had apparently been highly unprofessional, interfering with the film to the extent of forcing him to replace Kangana Ranaut (which he blamed on Dutt). He was simply adding to the growing dissent against Oberoi's tendency to meddle with Sanjay Dutt's scripts, films and relationships.

Interestingly, though he was vocal against both Dutt and Oberoi on Twitter, RGV and Sanjay Dutt eventually patched up and Oberoi officially became the villain of the piece. Following this, Oberoi filed a case in court against RGV on non-payments of dues amounting to ₹50 lakh for *Department*. He went a step further and asked for a stay on the release of RGV's next film, *Bhoot II*. The stay was refused by the Bombay High Court. Subsequently, Oberoi was sacked by Dutt, because there seemed to be far too many people who had issues with him.

But Oberoi was not the kind of man to go down quietly. Tabloids began to report that the real reason why he was kicked out was because he had been asked by Manyata to keep an eye on her philandering husband. She had found out that Dutt had been sowing his wild oats again and Oberoi had failed to report these incidents to her.

But there was more to Oberoi suddenly becoming persona non grata. At the time the controversy surfaced, he had been managing Kangana Ranaut's projects. The actress, who was not exactly known to be Ms Congeniality, was once pretty close to Manyata and even attended her baby shower. Mrs Dutt even reportedly helped Ranaut get a good deal on a property she wanted to buy but could not afford. Inexplicably, Manyata and Ranaut had a falling out. One school of thought claimed that this was probably why the actress was replaced in *Department*. Oberoi apparently messaged Kangana that he would not represent her any more, possibly choosing to side with his more influential clients. But it was not enough to save his job with the Dutts. After the film released, Oberoi was booted despite rumours that he and the Dutts may have patched up. Even though Sanjay Dutt was on a patch-up spree at the time, re-establishing connections, reports claimed that he was in a cold war situation with Oberoi circa October 2012. The two of them vied to remake the 1997 thriller *Inkaar* with their respective production houses. Oberoi had wanted to remake this film for a while and had even bought the rights from Raj Sippy when he was business manager for Sanjay. However, as it turned out, he had purchased the rights to use the film as a launch vehicle for his own production house. He had approached Anurag Basu to direct the remake. On the other hand, Dutt wanted to buy the rights to the film and also approached Raj Sippy for the same. To this day, the film remains unmade.

The Chhota Shakeel tapes set off a domino effect of sorts in Sanjay Dutt's world. While it was obvious that he had used his underworld connections to help the likes of Vidhu Vinod Chopra, who was being harassed by Abu Salem, he had also used the same connections to reign in his co-star, Govinda.

Govinda and Sanjay Dutt started their on-screen ride in 1989 with the film *Do Qaidi*. The two got along very well on and off the sets and made a popular comic pair in films like *Haseena Maan Jayegi*, *Jodi No.1* and *Ek Aur Ek Gyarah*. Their camaraderie made for a fun watch and industry insiders say they would constantly 'fool around on the sets and spend time in each other's vanity vans during breaks.'

Their bonhomie lasted even when they went through the rough

patches in their careers in 2000, with Govinda always gushing over 'Sanju baba' and boasting about their special relationship. 'He is a really misunderstood person,' he often said in interviews, defending him strongly. But everything changed when the tapes were released.

Outlook magazine wrote about the tapes:

> Film star Govinda too figures in the conversation, as does Hrithik Roshan, whose life seems to be under threat...
>
> The conversation is peppered with expletives and laughter.
>
> In the tape, Dutt also complains to Shakeel about actor Govinda's tantrums and not arriving on time for the shooting. Shakeel assures him that the matter would be taken care of.
>
> In this half-an-hour-long conversation, Sanjay Gupta and Harish Sugandh too chip in and director Mahesh Manjrekar says that he planned his next film on Shakeel's life.
>
> Manjrekar, who directed Dutt in *Vaastav*, a story about the underworld, tells Shakeel that he wants to make a film on his life, to which Shakeel says that he would chip in with inputs about, as well as his escape from Thailand. Even *Vastaav* was allegedly financed by underworld funds.
>
> In the tape, Harish tells Shakeel that he does not call up too often as the conversations are taped by the police.
>
> There is also a reference to the film *Devdas*, where Shakeel asks Harish about the film's financiers, including Bharat Shah.

The transcript and the expletives used for Govinda made headlines. The veteran actor was crushed. It was almost as if the younger actor had pulled a Jekyll and Hyde on him. One moment, they were enjoying their spot of bromance—and the next thing you know, Sanjay was ratting on Govinda to a dreaded mafia don. '*Dil ab khatta ho gaya na* (my heart has turned bitter)' Govinda said to a gathering of newspersons later. And when the hurt and anguish had given away to anger, he said, 'What can you expect from someone who doesn't even respect his own father? Sunilsaab is a "sant" (a saint), whilst Sanjay…'

The two actors barely managed to finish their last project together: David Dhawan's *Ek Aur Ek Gyarah*. *Masala* magazine wrote a detailed account of what transpired between the two stars on the set:

> Unit members said the two would sit in different corners of the sets in between shots. They would even have altercations since each insisted on giving a particular shot in his own way. Poor David Dhawan was often caught in the cross fire between Sanjay and Govinda. Once, when David and Chi Chi [Govidna] had a heated argument on filming a scene, Sanjay jumped in and defended the director. He even asked Govinda to stop being so stubborn! Sources say this interference from Sanjay was the last straw for Govinda who didn't want to hold back the bitterness and pain he had felt for too long. He is said to have retorted with harsh words and the result was an alleged verbal battle between the two actors in front of the unit.

Things just went from bad to worse for the two former buddies. *Ek Aur Ek Gyarah* worked at the box office, but it failed to give

Govinda's career the botox that it needed. His unprofessionalism was now on record—pun intended. He had pinned his hopes on a home production, *Shaadi Banaya*, starring Dutt in the lead. With the friendship now gone kaput, the film had to be shelved.

When Sanjay Dutt went to prison in 2007, Govinda apparently tried to reach out to him. One does not know why exactly Dutt refused to reciprocate. Was it ego? Or was it guilt? Govinda is still waiting for the answer.

*

Sanjay Dutt's complicated friendships are a hallmark of his life. And one such story is that of Salman Khan. Salman, every bit an awestruck kid, had modelled himself on the star—who was every boy's idol at that time. Long before Salman Khan became synonymous with the vest, the bare-chested look and the oversized turquoise studded bracelet; it was Sanjay Dutt who made it look good.

Salman and Sanjay were paired in one of the biggest hits of the time—*Saajan*, with Madhuri Dixit.

Salman had cast himself in the Dutt mould. He was inspired by the way Dutt had worked on his physique, his hairstyle and his swag. Both of them had an 'Alpha male' image going and both of them revelled in the whole bad boy persona. Salman hero-worshipped Dutt to such an extent that he was universally acknowledged as Sanjay Dutt version 2—or, Dutt minus the drugs. If Sanjay Dutt was Sanju Baba, he was Sallu Bhai. If Dutt was the Guru, Sallu was his chela. 'But I tell him, he should only pick the good things from me,' joked Dutt on a TV show once. The two Bad Boys of Bollywood even hosted a session of the *Bigg Boss* reality show, where Salman apparently chastised a contestant who had mocked Sanjay Dutt during one of the episodes.

Sanjay had a soft spot for Salman because Salim Khan had been instrumental in shaping Dutt's career in more ways than one. After all, he wrote him the career-defining *Naam*. Gratitude and affection for the younger, cleaner Mini Me version of Dutt is what defined this relationship for many years. Until it came down to—yes—egos.

At a time when Sanjay Dutt's career was in desperate need for some spin doctoring while he served the last leg of his sentence, Salman suggested that he sign up Reshma Shetty. After all, it was Shetty who had managed to turn Salman's professional life around and minted a squeaky clean public persona for the troubled star.

But reports suggest Sanjay was done waiting for Shetty to show some of her magic. And when nothing concrete or lucrative materialized, he dropped her. Salman, reportedly, was not happy with the way Reshma Shetty had been dismissed, leading to some bad vibes between him and Dutt.

The other version of the story traces the roots of the acrimony to the time when Salman was making *Bodyguard*. He wanted Sanjay Dutt to play the role of his father but Dutt didn't take this too kindly. He said in an interview: 'I am too young to play Salman's father.' Not surprisingly, it did not go down well with Khan.

The day Sanjay Dutt was released from prison, he first went to the Siddhi vinayak Temple with his wife Manyata and then came home to Imperial Heights. Almost everyone from the industry dropped by to welcome him back—except Salman Khan. Later, when Sanjay Dutt was asked on a show to describe his friends and colleagues with an adjective for each, he chose to describe Salman Khan as 'arrogant'. That really set tongues wagging—especially since, at a mutual friend's wedding, the two chose not to hang out with, or even acknowledge, each other. It was a sure sign that the long and deep friendship had suffered a serious blow. But as of now, they are back to being friends again—and even partied together recently in Spain.

★

One of his few friendships that seem to have survived unscathed is that with Ajay Devgn. Devgn's father, Veeru Devgan, is a legendary action director who had worked with Sanjay Dutt's father, Sunil Dutt. When he and Sunil Dutt worked together, Sanjay and Ajay would hang out on the sets. It is believed Kangana was treated badly by Dutt to help protect his buddy Devgn. According to a report in *Stardust*, Ajay Devgn and Kangana Ranaut were having a raging affair around this time. In the same sensational cover story, sources were quoted saying that Kangana insisted that Ajay had promised to marry her after his divorce with Kajol. The fact that she was willing to talk about the so-called affair riled Ajay Devgn to no end, and that is what got Sanjay Dutt to stand by him and make it truly difficult for Kangana Ranaut to find a toe-hold in the industry. Interestingly, Kangana was later seen in the Mata Ki Chowkis that Sanjay Dutt had organized after his release from prison. Apparently Manyata had insisted that they patch up again.

That Dutt would go to any length to help Devgn was evident when Kangana was not only dropped from *Department,* but was complete sidelined in *Rascals,* a film where she was supposed to be the female lead. While one would rarely find the two actors socializing in public, their friendship runs deeper than the paparazzi's reach. Devgn, known to be a fiercely private man, is famous for being a loner in the industry—although of late he has been in the news for his spats with the most influential Bollywood names (Karan Johar and Shah Rukh Khan). Dutt and Devgn have done some dud films together: *Raju Chacha, Tango Charlie, All the Best: Fun Begins, Rascals* and *Son Of Sardaar.* And none of their off-screen fondness for each other has translated to box office success.

In the media, on the rare occasions that the two hunks shared stage space, they had only the best things to say about each other:

'More than a friend, Ajay is like my brother… Raju (Ajay's pet name, which only a few people know of) gets comfortable with only a few people and I am a lucky guy to be his brother. And believe me, he is not at all as serious as he appears to be. I have seen him in his other elements. He is funny, extremely witty; he can come up with crazy one-liners instantaneously. He is a fun guy to be around.'

'Sanju and I are more than friends, we are like brothers. If I ask Sanju to do a film, he will not question me. If Sanju asks me to do a film, I will not question him. There are no favors or paybacks in my relationship with Sanju.'

'If someone comes to me and says Ajay did this or Ajay said this, I will never believe them because I trust my friend…we immediately call each other up to clarify things. There can never be any misunderstanding between us.'

Mahesh Bhatt is another person who stood by Dutt through thick and thin. Bhatt's *Naam* was one of the starting points of their long association and every time Dutt faced a personal crisis over his decades-old illegal arms possession case, Bhatt was always around. Whether it be Manyata or Kumar Gaurav or his sisters or Bunty Walia, Dutt has acknowledged the fact that whenever there was trouble, Bhatt always made that phone call. In fact, the first time he went behind bars for two months after coming back from Mauritius, the Dutt family was upset with the fact that none of the so-called industrywallahs bothered to even call them up or express solidarity—except a few like Mahesh Bhatt and Raj Babbar.

Bhatt and Sanjay Dutt's association blossomed during the making of *Sadak*. Bhatt's daughter, Pooja played the lead actress. Having grown up idolizing Sanjay Dutt, she spoke in interviews about how it was a big deal for her to be able to act opposite her childhood crush. Other than *Sadak* (1991) and *Naam* (1986), Bhatt made *Kabzaa* (1988), *Gumrah* (1993) and *Kartoos* (1999) with Dutt. After Sanjay Dutt walked out of prison, Pooja Bhatt posted a picture of Dutt and Bhatt engaged in a deep conversation, adding fuel to the speculation that *Sadak II* may be in the offing.

*

In one of the many interviews with Simi Garewal, Sanjay Dutt was asked if there was ever a phase in his life when things were 'normal'. He simply shook his head and said, 'no.' But the funny thing about Dutt is, despite the way he has often tempted fate, made mistakes and shot his mouth off, he has never been short of well-wishers. There has been no other star in the Indian film industry who has had as many brickbats from destiny as well as bouquets from his friends.

Even though Sanjay Dutt has often said that he has been disappointed by the lack of support from members of the film industry, the truth is, he was never really alone. The lack of visible support may have been out of fear—after all, his case had ticked all the wrong boxes: terror, politics, communalism, the underworld.

From the time he was sentenced, right through his incarceration and till the day he walked free, there were some people who not only put their faith in his innocence, but also fought for it. Sanjay, in an interview, thanked the likes of Shatrughan Sinha, who defied his party's stance and openly pleaded for his case. Amar Singh, his political mentor of over a decade, was another such person who used his powers to help Sanjay Dutt's cause as much as possible. Singh may have had political gains in mind, but he had reportedly been asked to intervene by the Bachchans, who, at one time, swore by Singh's ability to achieve the impossible. Both Amitabh and Abhishek have been particularly close to the Dutts. Abhishek paid Dutt a quiet visit the day he came home and has often spoken about their friendship. Jaya Prada and Jaya Bachchan both called for clemency while Subhash Ghai actually petitioned the governor to set Dutt free.

Ghai, who wanted to cast Sanjay as the lead in *Hero,* had cast him in a smaller role in the multistarrer *Vidhaata*. It was led by two veterans of the industry—Dilip Kumar and Shammi Kapoor.

This was in 1983 and Sanjay was in a permanent drug haze at the time, reporting late to work and earning the wrath of his seniors. Ghai was loathe to work with Sanjay again and *Hero* catapulted another actor to stardom—Jackie Shroff. Ghai waited for a decade till Sanjay actually cleaned up his act—and *Khalnayak* proved to be the biggest turning point in the actor's life.

Since then, Ghai has had a special place in his heart for Sanjay Dutt and continues to work on a script that will bring back the glory days of *Khalnayak* for his 'son'.

In 2002, Sanjay Dutt appeared on an episode of *Jeena Isi Ka Naam Hai,* hosted by veteran actor, the late Farooq Sheikh. The genteel, erudite and affable host introduced Dutt as someone he respected immensely, as 'with every challenge life throws his way, his stature only seems to get bigger.' In the episode, where key members of Dutt's family make an appearance, a message from the one person who was missing—Namrata—summed it all up: 'You have had many ups and downs in life and have always emerged stronger. There is a greater grace upon you… live your life well and remember—you are not alone.'

11

Films, Made and Not Made

Given that Sanjay Dutt has starred in no less than 190 films in his career spanning more than five decades, it comes as no surprise that the star has both some great and some embarrassing work to his credit.

In a *Stardust* article titled 'Isn't Sanjay Dutt the Real Angry Young Man?' the writer analyzes the root of Sanjay Dutt's infamous anger. He speaks of an incident where Sanjay was driving a white Fiat, when a car from the opposite direction headed straight towards him. He swerved sharply and avoided a head-on crash. He cursed and drove on towards his friend's place. He had just driven into the compound and parked, when a car screeched to a halt in front of his. It was the same car that had almost crashed into his. The driver staggered out and started hurling abuses at him. He was obviously drunk. The driver had barely slammed the door shut when Sanjay was upon him. A blow on the mouth cut him off mid-sentence. Several more followed. His mouth was bleeding and he had a deep gash on the left cheek when Sanjay shoved him into the car and said, 'Go away, before I kill you.' This is not a scene from his films, but a real incident. But this persona has been reflected repeatedly on-screen, in his movies.

Jaan Ki Baazi was one of Sanjay Dutt's first films after his drug detox, where he is seen destroying anything and everything that comes his way. Even in his other release, *Naam*, the inherent threat is always implied. The audience is never allowed to get that they're watching a potentially violent man. In the opening reels of the film, Dutt tells a ruffian in a relatively jovial tone to stay out of his way. He goes on to show him his fists and when the toughie begins to get rough, he lands one on his face, sending him reeling. Later, in the film, when Dutt decides to give up drug peddling and turn a new leaf, the kingpin refuses to let him go. In a confrontation scene that can be quite chilling depending on your state of mind, the Mafioso tells him not to leave if he fears for his life. The camera freezes on his face as Dutt replies—'The only thing I am afraid of is my anger.'

The message hits home. In *Jeeva*, he is all blood and fury because, in the film, his parents have been burned alive. In *Mera Haque*, he keeps himself in check through a large part of the film, but in the fight sequence at the climax, he is violent. In *Naam O Nishan*, he plays a police inspector who takes on the underworld.

Dutt has always felt that he has been typecast as the action hero. But he has confessed that he had a violent streak—especially in his drug haze phase, when he would often be violent without reason. He often showed people he trusted his weapon collection—kukris, guns and swords. Did he ever realise that his obsession with weapons would come back to haunt him and ruin his life one day? Sanjay Dutt has never been the kind of person known for his/her pragmatism or foresight.

He states that at least on two occasions, he went around taking potshots at innocent passersby outside his father's bungalow, just for kicks. And that too with a big bore rifle—which could even kill. Eventually, the cops had to persuade him to stop and his gun licence was revoked.

Comparisons between Dutt and Bachchan truly started after the release of *Naam*. The character he played was on the wrong side of law. He was also the underdog. The film's writer, Salim Khan, said at the time that his intention was anything but to make him like the character he wrote for Bachchan. 'He is not an angry young man,' Khan said to *Stardust*. 'He is physically strong but is vulnerable and confused. Bachchan was very confident. He could look after himself in films like *Zanjeer* and *Deewar*. This character needs guidance and support.' Once again, very close to real life.

The characters Bachchan played were very unexpressive in showing their love for a girlfriend or a brother or a mother. But in *Naam*, Dutt is very fond of his brother, played by Kumar Gaurav, and shows it. What Salim Khan didn't mention are the scenes in *Naam* that were tailormade for Bachchan. There is one where Dutt talks about being afraid of his anger. A scene shows a subway where the hero is being confronted by a band of armed hoodlums. Dutt tells them he knows that they can overpower him, but the first man who touches him would soon be dead. With Bachchan, the scene would have been much more intense, like in *Deewar,* when he walks into a warehouse full of villains, locks the door, throws away the key and says he will take it out of the villain's pocket. The parallels were evident.

Whether for the two song and dance sequences in *Jeeva,* or for *Mera Haque,* where Dutt resembled Bachchan in the long shots and some of the drunken comic scenes that were Big B's speciality, the two were being compared.

Dutt was being nudged into playing the kind of roles that Bachchan had played in his prime. With the physical build that he inherited from his father and the good looks that he got from his mother, Dutt was essentially a combination of the best of both sides. Add to that the whole dark brooding act, the droopy eyes and a history that was equally dark—and perhaps enticing for some—and you had a winning combination.

During the outdoor shooting of *Hathyar,* large crowds gathered on the bridge under which the unit was shooting. When Sanjay Dutt arrived, there was a deafening roar of delight. Prakash Mehra, who had produced *Imandaar* and *Mohabbat Ke Dushman* (which he had also directed), was betting big on Sanjay Dutt.

Dutt lacked depth in his expressions. In some scenes in *Naam,* he looks vaguely lost in moments when he should be glowering. In *Masihaa* and *Ganga Bahet Rahi,* Sunil Dutt tried to coach Sanjay. There was a lot of hope and there were a lot of expectations of Sanjay Dutt—not only because of who he was, but because he was the kind of package that was rare in those days. After Bachchan, there had been no one who could match up to his stature.

But where did all this goodwill and fan following, this craze around Sanjay Dutt, go? Was he responsible for the industry turning against him and his family, or was the industry just being selfish in refusing to stand by him? Or was it that Dutt was never really meant to be an actor? He was just a star-kid with a certain image that seemed to have a charm and raw sex appeal. His looks were very unlike what Bollywood had seen for the longest time. His body was built at the gym, very rare in those days. Until that point, there were very few male leads who had worked on their physique the way he had.

The 80s

While films such as *Rocky* and *Naam* will be remembered as his biggest turning points in the early years, there are some other films that went onto define his image—both on-screen and off it.

When Sanjay Dutt returned from America after treatment, he went on a film-signing spree with *Naam, Hathyar* and *Jaan Ki Baazi* etc. *Jaan Ki Baazi* was his first release post rehab and action director Pappu Verma turned producer with this film, while Ajay Kashyap made his debut as director. *Jaan Ki Baazi* was successful, perhaps because Dutt was eager to prove his mettle. He exuded tremendous energy on screen and endeared himself to his fans all over again. His pairing with Anita Raj, too, seemed to be work. Those were simplistic days of filmmaking and the audiences were not very hard to please.

In 1984, Dutt frontlined a rather peculiar film called *Zameen Aasman*. He had signed this film right after *Rocky* and Anita Raj, who was a newcomer at that time, was supposed to star alongside him. Thanks to his unpredictable ways, the film was delayed by a good few years. The film also starred veterans Rakhee, Rekha and Shashi Kapoor and the plot had all the possible tropes and cliches you could imagine in a Bollywood film: unrequited love, a love triangle, misunderstandings and a young couple keen to elope. It was a truly forgettable film—had it not been for the bizarre rumours of Rekha having an affair with Dutt. The media reported that Rekha may have secretly tied the knot with the handsome youngster. So strong were the rumours, that Dutt has to issue an official statement denying it.

Khatron Ke Khiladi, starring Dharmendra as the honest truck driver with a vendetta meting out justice, mob style, had Dutt playing his son. The film generated plenty of controversy thanks to the gossip emanating from the set. During the filming of a song, director T. Rama Rao and Sanjay Dutt got into a major argument. Sanjay was not getting a dance move right. T. Rama Rao abused Sanjay, saying that his mother Nargis was such a graceful dancer and Sanjay 'was worse than a piece of wood.' He thundered, 'Who made him an actor?' Sanjay stormed off the sets, promising never to work with Rao again. It was also during this film that he met Madhuri Dixit.

In 1988, Sanjay Dutt also starred in Prakash Mehra's *Mohabbat Ke Dushman*. He was simply overshadowed by the towering Raaj Kumar and Hema Malini combine, while he romanced Farha Naaz to little effect. Perhaps Sanjay Dutt was still dealing with rage and ego issues and there were plenty of reports about how he and the veteran Kumar had several arguments over the most explosive lines. According to film gossip, the senior star was apparently threatened by the charismatic youngster. The latter was in no mood to cede any footage to the former.

The 90s

Having survived some of the biggest personal crises till date, the '90s saw Sanjay Dutt finally finding his feet in the industry.

The decade began on a good note with *Thanedaar,* starring Jeetendra, Jaya Prada and Madhuri Dixit in the lead roles, with music composed by Bappi Lahiri. The song 'Tamma Tamma Loge', that went on to become a hit, had a wooden Sanjay Dutt shaking a leg (or trying to) with the stunning Dixit, who moved like a dream on the dance floor. The song, however, proved to the undoing of Sanjay Dutt's friendship with Mukul S. Anand—for a bit. Choreographer Saroj Khan, who had watched the rushes of the sensational song 'Jumma Chumma' from Mukul Anand's *Hum,* pictured on Amitabh Bachchan and Kimi Katkar, alerted the *Thanedaar* team about the potential blockbuster. They responded by getting Lahiri to replicate a tune originally composed by *Guinean vocalist Mory Kanté,* set to different and safer lyrics. But Saroj Khan was so sure that Sanjay Dutt would not be able to match steps with Dixit, she used a body double for some of the scenes. Apparently it was Javed Jaffrey's feet that did the trick. But Mukul Anand could not get over the slight and even though *Hum* turned out to be that year's biggest hit, his friendship with Sanjay Dutt soured.

Around the same time, S Dutt was supposed to star in Anand's ambitious *Khuda Gawah* as inspector Raja Mirza, with Amitabh Bachchan and Sridevi. But he dropped out of the project after shooting some of his scenes. The star alleged that Mukul had wasted seventy days of his schedule, while the director claimed permissions for shooting in Afghanistan delayed the project. Some reports claimed that after Big B's smashing performance in *Hum*—where even Rajinikanth and Govinda were completely overshadowed—Sanjay Dutt was unsure of how his role would turn out. The truth was somewhere in between.

It was the bitter aftertaste of the Tamma-Jumma controversy that marred the association. Anand had fired Saroj Khan from *Khuda Gawah* after he figured out her role in the controversy. Sanjay Dutt simply opted out, rather than deal with the inevitable awkwardness.

The two came together again in an ill-fated project that could change Bollywood for ever. Known to be 'thick as thieves' and inspiring each other to use their 'body as work', Salman Khan and Sanjay Dutt were the top draws in *Dus*—a slick Hollywood-style action thriller by the flamboyant Anand.

'In May 1997, the two stars had begun shooting for the film about two Indian secret agents who are sent on a mission to Afghanistan to capture the terrorist Nasheman, played by Raveena Tandon. The lavishly mounted film was being touted as a breakthrough in Indian cinema in terms of Hollywood-level stunts, and it would have been further proof of the style and pizzazz that the director of *Agneepath,*

Hum and *Khuda Gawah* brought to the screen. The actors were being brought together after a hit pairing as inseparable brothers in *Saajan* (1991). Composers Shankar Ehsaan Loy were making their feature film debut with *Dus*, and all the elements were in place for a blockbuster,' wrote Manish Gaekwad on Scroll.in.

On 7 September 1997, Anand died of a heart attack, 'leaving the project incomplete and in the hands of his wife Anita Anand.'

In an interview with Scroll.in, Anita Anand, the bereaved wife of Mukul, said: 'Mukul Anand started writing the film almost two years before he began filming it… His first choice for the role was Salman Khan and Sanjay Dutt as he wrote the script with them in mind. Stunt teams from America were hired, cameras in crash boxes [were placed] right in front of the car. He was using all sorts of technology I couldn't grasp. The funniest was when Salman and Sanjay were hanging from the helicopters and flying across. They were harnessed but it was still highly dangerous. They were abusing Mukul throughout, but it was all in fun.'

Saajan and *Sadak*, both releasing in 1991, marked one of Sanjay Dutt's career highs. He was yet to be affected by the arms controversy and having survived a broken marriage, fatherhood and bereavement, he seemed to focus all his energies into his work. And it showed.

Directed by Lawrence D'Souza, *Saajan* revolved around Aman (Sanjay), Akash (Salman Khan) and Pooja (Madhuri Dixit) and was complete formula stuff, with the story of a friendship between the orphaned and disabled Aman and the wealthy Akash. But the script had plenty of punch and the songs were successful. Sanjay

Dutt, who hobbled on a walking stick, became a style icon with his lanky hair and OTT blazers with extra padded shoulders. The film ran for seventy-five weeks at the box office. It had a diamond jubilee celebration and catapulted both Sanjay Dutt and Khan into the A-league of Bollywood. *Saajan* became the highest grossing film of 1991, shattering all previous box office records and establishing itself as the fifth highest grosser of the '90's. In 1991, *Saajan*'s gross box office collection was ₹15 crores, which adjusted to today, stands at ₹181.70 crore. The net collection was ₹7.50 crore which, adjusted to today, stands at ₹90.85 crore.

Audiences that had so far been accustomed to watching a wooden Sanjay Dutt essay macho roles that required little else but to flex his muscles, were surprised with his attempts at emoting. As the heartbroken poet, he managed to capture the isolation and quiet despair of a lonely figure. His character was vulnerable, fragile and almost apologetic—a far cry from his boisterous character in *Thanedaar* the previous year, in which he had played to the gallery. It also raised the question—was this the real Sanjay Dutt?

Sadak, directed by Mahesh Bhatt, starred Dutt in a pivotal role alongside Pooja Bhatt. Dutt showed some rare maturity in his work and Pooja gave a round of interviews in which she expressed equal delight—she was finally paired with the star who had been her first crush.

With enough action, blood and an unusual villain—Sadashiv Amrapurkar, playing a transgender person—*Sadak* ticked all the boxes of a surefire hit. Add to it songs that were melodious and the impish girl-woman played by Pooja Bhatt, who was a teen sensation at that time. Sanjay Dutt played a dark, brooding character tormented by memories of his sister's traumatic death and driven by an innate desire to do good—a taxi driver with fists of fury and a heart of gold. The climactic scene, where he is crucified and left for dead, left audiences in frenzy and sent the makers laughing all the way to the bank.

Exactly two years later, Sanju's life changed forever. He returned from Mauritius to be arrested at the airport itself.

We all know about how Subhash Ghai's *Hero* launched the career of Jackie Shroff. But the fact that it could also have been a career-defining role for Sanjay Dutt is rarely discussed. In retrospect, it was a role that had Sanjay Dutt written all over it. And Shroff rose to the challenge, styling himself like a cleaner version of the drug-addled star-son—the same wild hair, dreamy eyes, rakish charm and a swag that seemed oh-so-charming. Dutt lost out on *Hero* thanks to his antics during the shoot of *Vidhaata*. But Ghai made up for the miss, and how. Providence and canny marketing came together when, ten years later, Ghai created *Khalnayak* for Dutt. In several interviews, he spoke of how the boy with the golden heart was actually misunderstood and how a little bit of tender loving care (read Madhuri Dixit) could have actually reined him in. Made in the thick of the arms possession controversy, Sanjay Dutt's *Khalnayak* was a nudge and wink to reality. As a roguish Dutt sang to the camera, '*Nayak nahin, khalnayak hoon main* (I'm not the hero, I'm the villain),' the audiences erupted. All across the country, giant cutouts of the 'Khalnayak' were festooned and worshipped. Baba was the guru of the masses, who began to sport his long hairstyle and mimicked his peculiar body movements from the film. It helped to have another raunchy number in the mix ('Choli Ke Peeche') and there was enough juicy controversy to drive the film to its box office goals.

Khalnayak released in the same year as *Sahibaan,* where he was a prince in sumptuous clothes. What a contrast.

Mahesh Bhatt once said—and rightly so—that there is perhaps no other actor who cares so little about looking good in a movie. *Khalnayak* was perhaps one such film where the actor willingly donned the grease paint—quite literally. His scruffy look and the wild hair covering half his face, his piercing gaze and peculiar grin, were completely over the top and completely Bollywood. The character Ballu's trajectory—from a young boy to a hardened criminal who rekindles his inner humanity thanks to Ganga—resonated with the audiences at that most appropriate moment. Ballu was Baba. Baba was Ballu. And Ghai was not complaining.

Two years later, when Sanjay Gupta's *Aatish* released, Dutt was seen toting machine guns. Even though the shadow of the court case was very much looming over him, he showed off his muscle power in the film that is best remembered for launching Gupta's trademark genre of guns and guys. If it was politically incorrect, it did not matter. Dutt looked at home in the role and the film went on to be a success.

The late 90s saw Sanjay Dutt star in a string of forgettable films until, in 1999, *Vaastav* more than made up for the misadventures. His portrayal of a young man drawn into the underworld was stunning. Mahesh Manjrekar's directorial debut was celebrated for its dialogues and screenplay, and the film enjoys a cult status today. Sanjay Dutt was nominated for the Filmfare Best Actor Award for the fourth time in his then eighteen-year-old film career and finally won it. The role is unanimously regarded by critics as being one of Indian cinema's most memorable and most quoted on-screen characters.

Once again, Sanjay Dutt's character Raghubir teased his own past. Not only was the character supposedly inspired by Chhota Rajan, someone he allegedly knew only too well, the scene where his mother pulls the trigger on her rogue son and then cradles him in her arms, reminded audiences of a similar scene in *Mother India* featuring his parents Nargis and Sunil Dutt.

In several interviews, Sanjay Dutt spoke of the final scene as one of his best. It was shot in two takes. Two cameras were used—one inside the house and one outside. He also spoke of how he was hugely inspired by Al Pacino's performance in *Scarface* (1983) and felt that he wanted to bring it alive in his own way in Bollywood. With a stellar supporting cast picked from Marathi theatre, the film was on solid ground and was the much-needed 'comeback' for the actor, who had just emerged from a jail term and a career low.

The year also brought him a modicum of comic relief with *Haseena Maan Jayegi*, an out-and-out slapstick comedy co-starring Govinda, although it was Govinda who walked away with the awards and recognition for what was to be one of his best roles in a long time to come.

The New Millennium

Sanjay Dutt's serious streak continued into the new millennium with Vidhu Vinod Chopra's *Mission Kashmir*. It was a complex, nuanced role and had it not been for the tone set by *Vaastav* earlier, no one would have believed that Dutt would be able to carry it off.

There is an interesting backstory to this sensitive film about Kashmiriyat and terrorism. Apparently, Amitabh Bachchan was supposed to play the role of Inayat Khan, the cop who adopts a terrorist's child. Bachchan opted out since he was doing *Moahabbatein* that year with Yash Raj Films.

After roping in Sanjay Dutt for the role of Khan, Vinod signed up Hrithik Roshan who was the flavour of the moment thanks to the sensational success of *Kaho Naa... Pyar Hai*.

Once on board, Roshan's role was amplified to that of a second lead, almost overshadowing Khan. Chopra could take this liberty because of his close bond with Sanjay Dutt, who was always happy to play the smallest of roles for him. Even then, the step down must not have been easy for the actor, who was hungry to prove himself all over again. He delivered a powerful performance as the older man, reducing Roshan to a pretty face with a rippling six pack. The final showdown between the two stars packed in enough firepower to keep critics happy and the audiences impressed.

In his book *Maximum City*, Suketu Mehta wrote about the film and its impact:

> At a screening at Rashtrapati Bhavan for the President of India [...] The columnist Ali Peter John interviews the actor for the Screen...
>
> Sanjay: I couldn't for the life of me believe that I who was considered and is still considered a criminal by the court was invited by the President of India himself. I also started believing that the high powers in the land were aware that I was innocent, caught in a trap, built by my enemies... It was my greatest moment when the President, Mr Narayanan, shook my hands and patted me. I slept that night like I have never slept before. India loved me. The people of India wanted all the best things to happen to me. They were willing to give me all the love I asked for.

In 2002, Sanjay Dutt teamed up with his buddy Sanjay Gupta to form White Feather Films and their first baby was a glossy, heavily stylized rendition of *Reservoir Dogs. Kaante,* starring an all-star cast of Amitabh Bachchan, Sanjay Dutt, Kumar Gaurav, Mahesh Manjrekar, Suniel Shetty and Lucky Ali, packed enough firepower to blast its way through the box office.

Kaante was one of Quentin Tarantino's favourites from the myriad films that were 'inspired' by his work. He praised the film for fleshing out its characters, beyond what he could achieve in *Reservoir Dogs*. He said in an interview with short film director Srinivas at the Indian Film Festival in Los Angeles: 'Here I am, watching a film that I've directed and then it goes into each character's background. And I'm like, "Whoa". For, I always write backgrounds and stuff and it always gets chopped off during the edit. And so I was amazed on seeing this. I felt, this isn't *Reservoir Dogs*. But then it goes into the warehouse scene and I am like, "Wow, it's back to *Reservoir Dogs*." Isn't it amazing!'

Kaante was literally a film based on friendships and gratitude. While Sanjay Dutt pulled out all the stops for his buddy Gupta, the other actors were all there because of him. Amitabh Bachchan never forgot that Sunil Dutt had once given him a big chance with the role of Chhotu in *Reshma Aur Shera* when he was still a newcomer in the film industry. He was simply returning the favour. Director Mahesh Manjrekar was in it for his friend Sanju Baba, who had helped him take *Vaastav* to stratospheric levels. Singer Lucky Ali and Suniel Shetty were all friends with Sanjay Dutt while Kumar Gaurav was simply in it for his brother-in-law and oldest friend.

But all the men in black were no match for the electrifying presence of Bachchan and Dutt. They seemed to feed off of each other's energy and Sanjay Dutt rocked the cool, slick baddie as though he was born to play him. As Ajju, he presented himself, for the first time, in the look and the kind of role he is cut out for, which he would extend and refine in later films like *Plan* or *Musafir*: the cool macho gangster, one step ahead of his bhais (not without reason did he get the Bollywood Movie Critics Award and another Filmfare nomination for Best Supporting Actor for the role).

The other interesting thing about *Kaante* was Sanjay Dutt's mature sex appeal. His cool swagger was evident in the song 'Ishq Samunder'. He continued in the same tone with *Plan*'s 'Pyaar Aaya' and *Musafir*'s 'Saaki Saaki'. He seemed to get better both as the don and the dancer.

The following year, *Munna Bhai M.B.B.S.* happened. The rest, to use a cliche, is history.

The professional highs that Sanjay Dutt experienced at this time predictably slumped for the next couple of years, till 2005. His friend Vidhu Vinod Chopra came to his rescue once again with a film he produced for debutant director Pardeep Sarkar. *Parineeta,* starring Vidya Balan and Saif Ali Khan in the lead, had Sanjay Dutt play the role of Girish—the warm compassionate friend of Lalita, the female protagonist, in this adaptation of Sarat Chandra Chattopadhyay's novel. It was not the kind of role one would expect a macho action star to play. But once again, Dutt went for broke. And the results were more than satisfying as he impressed critics and audiences with his subtle performance in the nuanced role.

This was also the year Anubhav Sinha paid a tribute to Mukul Anand with *Dus,* a spy thriller about the anti-terrorism squad, starring Sanjay Dutt in the lead. The film had little else in common with the original, unfinished production, but was a roaring success with its slick action sequences.

From 2005 to 2012, except for the *Munna Bhai* sequel, Sanjay Dutt's career seemed to limp on. There were some travesties in the name of comic capers—especially *Rascals*—and had it not been for *Agneepath,* things would have unravelled completely for the star battling an intensifying court case and age.

Mukul Anand's towering *Agneepath* is not the kind of film that anyone would have had the gumption to revisit. But Karan

Johar had just the right kind of audacity of ambition and debutant Karan Malhotra was the right person to helm the blood-and-gore tribute to the original. While Hrithik Roshan did his darndest best as the protagonist, he was no match for the two supervillains—Rishi Kapoor as Rauf Lala and Sanjay Dutt as Kancha Cheena. While Kapoor obviously relished his villainous turn and came up with a highly original take on the character of a cold, shrewd, slimy flesh trader, Kancha was something else. Even after Dutt's multiple outings as memorable baddies, this was exceptional. He used his physicality to superb effect, showing off his carefully and diligently tended muscles and tattoos in flowing black robes, shaved off his head and wore and summoned all the possible dark energies to chillingly portray a character reminiscent of Darth Vader and Voldemort. Kancha was the millennials' answer to Gabbar and Mogambo: A madman who lives by his own version of the *Bhagavad Gita* and ruthlessly uses and suppresses people for his own purposes.

His natural propensity for brutality and his blood-curdling grin set the stage for the dramatic action sequences. According to reports, Sanjay apparently asked for a break while dubbing for the film because he couldn't stand himself anymore and was seriously wondering whether the monster on the screen was really him.

The audiences may or may not have loved the remake, but there was no holding back their love for Sanjay Dutt, who astonished everyone once again with his ability to immerse himself in roles as diverse as Munna and Kancha. In an interview with *The Times of India*, he said:

I am overwhelmed at the reactions for *Agneepath*. I visited some popular single screen theatres and was taken aback by the audience's response! I was stunned when they started whistling and clapping at my entry. The noise was deafening. I felt on top of the world! I never expected such big opening collections either. People have complimented me on my range as an actor—that I can play both the lovable Munna Bhai and the horrible Kancha with ease. It's a very good feeling to be praised like that. When you work hard and get such tremendous appreciation from both fans and friends, you feel a real sense of achievement.

12

Style Bhai

As the first star-son to command his unique identity—as far removed as possible from that of his illustrious parents—and fan following and narrative, by design and by destiny, Sanjay Dutt's real and reel image deserve a close scrutiny through the prism of his public persona.

To put things in context: In 1981, when Dutt exploded onto the scene with *Rocky,* he was unlike any other actor Bollywood had seen so far. He was lanky, droopy eyed, wore his hair long and was distinctly 'westernized' in his slim pants, bomber jackets with his initials emblazoned on it and pulling stunts on his bike. No one seemed to care that he was evidently ill-equipped to emote; his reckless rock star aura simply filled up the screen.

The same year, another star-son made his debut—Sanjay Dutt's buddy Kumar Gaurav. He was the ultimate dream boat in a romantic film, and even if both the boys shared the same youthful vibe—a departure from the flock of veterans ruling the marquee at that time—they were as different as chalk and cheese.

Kumar Gaurav went on to become the most famous example of a one-hit wonder, trapped in his own image—a soft-spoken goody two shoes. Sanjay Dutt seemed to challenge his own image with every outing. The relentless focus on his personal life and the high expectations from each one of his films may have also played a part. But the fact is, no other male actor has had the kind of an influence on the audiences and on his peers that Dutt did. And we are not talking about his acting chops here.

Over the years, Sanjay Dutt perpetuated and perfected the rakish, gangsta, rockstar look and owned the deadly Dutt monicker that the media had gifted him. The lanky, dopey-eyed image ran its course and post his rehab stint, Dutt returned to a different world order. In 1983, another star-son, Sunny Deol, had made his debut. Unlike Sanjay Dutt's troubled legacy, Deol was squeaky clean. His debut was *Betaab*, a film that had turned him into an overnight star. And with every successive outing, Deol was flexing his genetic muscles, endearing himself to the masses. The slot of the tough guy with a soft heart and a clear conscience was taken. There was only one option left for Sanjay Dutt—get tougher. And show off.

The first of Sanjay Dutt's many reinventions came with his sculpted body. Deol was obviously fit. But Dutt was ready to flaunt his ripped muscles. He wore his hair long and a cigarette always dangled from his lips. In most of his photo shoots he appeared reckless, wore the occasional frown and dared to appear only in his vest, showing off his hairy chest (that eventually made way for a smoother one)—perhaps the first male actor to do so.

Throughout the late '80s and '90s, Sanjay Dutt was our version of James Dean—a rebel without a cause—and Sylvester Stallone put together. He was the guy who could tame the wildest of mares and meanest of machines and wore leather jackets and ripped denims as though he was born into them. But just before you thought he was getting comfortable in his image, he would surprise you with a delightful willingness to throw it all away for something starkly different.

From the ganji in *Aatish* to the padded blazers in *Saajan*; from the wild, maniacal locks in *Khalnayak* to the slick hairdo and white pathan suit in *Vaastav*; from the hip urban suits in *Shabd* to the chilling hairless villain in *Agneepath,* he has always displayed a willingness to immerse himself into the character in his own way. Even in some of the loudest David Dhawan comedies, where his comic timing may have found full play, he seems to ace Govinda in the sartorial department, indulging in kitschy, over the top outfits befitting the genre. He had a total disregard for looking photogenic on screen—which no other A-list actor or star has ever dared. It was his brand of method acting, long before the Aamir Khans of the world appropriated the space with a certain sophistication. What has remained constant, however, are Sanjay Dutt's muscles: his body, his temple and his penance. Even while he experimented wildly with his outfits and his hairstyles, he never, ever let go of his body. The body was Dutt; Dutt was the body.

In 2015, when Sanjay Dutt was serving his sentence at the

Yerwada Jail in Pune, he stepped out for a fourteen-day parole. The moment he stepped out to face the gaggle of camerapersons, he rolled up his vest to everyone's shock and surprise. It seemed his ripped abs were back. Dutt, who worked out rigorously in jail, seemed to have lost weight and seemed fitter than before. When asked about it, he told Zee News Service, 'Yes, I have lost 18 kilos in jail. I had made six packs and now I will make eight packs.'

It was certainly not an easy task.

Right before he stepped into Yerwada, Dutt was battling a bulge. On a TV show, where he appeared with Manyata, he was ribbed on for his excess weight and Manyata did not take it well. Once inside, according to reports, Dutt replaced his usual dumb bells with spades and trash buckets filled with water. He got so used to the regime that even after his jail term, he stopped using his regular gym equipment and preferred to use props and articles that were more easily available. Apparently he replaced all strength training exercises, such as bicep curls, with functional exercises. His trainer, Sunil Prabhale, has been quoted in media reports saying, 'Irrespective of where he is, Dutt never skips his workout session and follows a very strict high protein diet.'

For someone who started the trend of gym buddies—him, Suniel Shetty, Salman Khan and even Hrithik Roshan during *Agneepath*—the body was sacrosanct, and a perfectly sculpted body could actually fight the demons of his mind. The fittest of action stars before him, such as Dharmendra, never had a personal trainer. But Dutt changed all that. His team of personal trainers and tattoo- and hairstylists turned into overnight stars in their own fields, thanks to the tremendous influence he wielded on his peers and his fans.

Speaking about his formula, Dutt said at a press conference:

> I am also doing martial arts. Gym and diet is a science. You have to do it according to that. The metabolic rate decreases and you gotta increase that. That is what we basically do. I have also stopped drinking. The diet also has to be quite strict. My diet usually has grilled fish, grilled chicken and boiled vegetables.
>
> Acting, I think, it comes in the course of time and as you mature. I think it's the same thing with bodybuilding. You get into it, work out, make mistakes, train with people and learn. That's how you do it. Twenty-five years back, Bombay had only one gym. So I had to build my own gym. There is no age limit for bodybuilding. If you look at Mr Sylvester Stallone, at this age to have such a great physique is amazing. It's just your dedication and how you do it. My way of looking at bodybuilding for actors is different. In every movie you cannot take your shirt off. You have to plan a movie where it is necessary that your shirt is off and people get a shock when they see you. You gotta shock your audience. So every two minutes if you are gonna take your shirt off it doesn't matter.
>
> After I got out of jail, it took about a year to get back into shape. Come what may, every day, from 6 to 8 in the evening is my workout time. Come what may, I do not miss that.

Now, not many people know that the person who introduced Dutt to bodybuilding was an actor who was seen in villainous roles, usually as a henchman or a sidekick to the main villain, in 90s Bollywood. He was an Indian actor of Irish origin called Gavin Packard and he acted with Dutt in films such as *Sadak*.

Gavin was a professional bodybuilder who had won various state and national bodybuilding championships. Dutt was always known to be a rather lanky actor, at least till before the time he went to the US for his drug rehab. After he came back from rehab, he seriously started to work on his body and set the standard for the male physique in Bollywood. He had Packard to thank for it. Packard was mentoring not just him but also his friends Suniel Shetty and Salman Khan after him. When he passed away at the age of forty-eight, Dutt was quoted as saying, 'He was like a brother to me. He introduced me to body building.' Apparently Dutt remained close to Packard's family and was a godfather to his children.

In the book, *Fashioning Bollywood: The Making and Meaning of Hindi Film Costume,* the author Clare M. Wilkinson explains in the chapter, 'From Style to Power: The Hero Body', how the Bollywood hero stereotype has changed over the years. She writes how the men were not 'remarkable' in their physicality in the initial days of Bollywood. Either the men were clothed or they were the likes of Dara Singh in the '50s and '60s—more of an exception than the rule. With the advent of hand-to-hand fighting in the action films of the 70s, there emerged a new hero, whose body needed to look credibly strong. Dharmendra exemplified this shift in perception. It was given a more perceptive edge with Amitabh Bachchan, who used his limbs and his height to convey machismo. Writes Wilkinson:

By the 1980s and 1990s, however, a strong, muscular body had become a more common, and, ultimately a normative dimension of the hero's persona. It is no accident that Bollywood heroes of the 1980s and the 1990s cite Sylvester Stallone as a major inspiration. Dharmendra's son Sunny Deol continued in his father's footsteps, with a career largely based upon roles in action films. Among the first stars to use body building to craft a precisely muscled body, was Sanjay Dutt... son of Nargis and Sunil Dutt. Shortly after, Salman Khan installed the prevailing standard for the contemporary hero in the 1990s...

Between them, Sanjay Dutt and Salman Khan have set a standard of male body discipline that persists, and indeed has expanded (like so many chests), today. Surveying the parade of magnificently muscled creatures who auditioned for the part of Jamal in 2008's *Slumdog Millionaire,* director Danny Boyle lamented that he couldn't find a single young Indian actor with a body that could convey the vulnerability he wanted for the character. He had to turn to Dev Patel, an actor from Britain, where the superlatively toned body is not yet the gold standard of masculinity. Decades after British colonists derided the nakedness of the Indians as inconsistent with their own notion of a matured, authoritative masculinity, there is a fairly rich irony here.

The carefully toned and cultivated body can be as singular an attribute of the star as the face, a phenomenon strikingly put to use in Ashutosh Gowarikar's *Jodha Akbar.*

It is difficult to explain why and how Sanjay Dutt became the style icon that he did for his peers, for the upcoming youngsters in Bollywood and for hundreds and thousands of men in the country. If you look back, the hairstyle that he sported was not exactly attractive—but it was sensational. No one else before him had dared to wear it long and colour it at will. His style has swung from the cool to the outrageous and everything else in between.

In his earliest days, Dutt wore his hair pretty much in the way all young men of that time wore it—a variation of the Amitabh Bachchan cut, with longish hair covering the ears. Post rehab, he seemed to struggle with a receding hairline and his naturally straight, silky hair was perhaps best suited for a kind of mullet—short in the front and long at the back. Through some of his most successful years—*Sadak, Saajan* and *Thaanedar*—Dutt's mullet was a trailblazer and was the new Bachchan cut for youngsters of the time. The mullet turned into a mess of wild long hair in films such as *Daud,* with a distinctively golden touch and just black and wild in *Khalnayak.* He even went platinum blonde in one of his gangsta flicks.

In films such as *Musafir* and *Luck,* Dutt had his favourite stylist Aalim Hakim create sculpted sideburns and a moustache. *Lamha* saw him look completely different in salt and pepper hair and a scraggy beard. In *Vaastav,* the blazing red tika on his sprawling forehead was in focus with the slick, gelled-back hair, while he embraced his inner rastafarian in *Kartoos.* It was all about sophistication in *Shabd,* where he swapped his biker gang persona for crisp suits and a close crop. *Zinda* had him wear a hard hairdo and facial fuzz while *Kaante* saw a sharp French cut and matching crop. *Zanjeer* had Dutt replicate Praan's iconic look, complete with a full-blown beard, while *Son of Sardaar* saw him sport an OTT 'stache.

But nothing quite prepared his fans for his spine-chilling look in *Agneepath* as Kancha Cheena. His full blown biceps and tattoos on display in the billowy black satin robes, his head tonsured and eyebrows and chest shaved, ears heavily accessorized—Dutt was Voldemort in a desi avatar. Interestingly, even as he was shooting for *Agneepath,* he turned up for *Rascals* with a stylish crop. According to a *Mumbai Mirror* article:

> It wasn't any wonder drug for hair growth, but a special wig created in LA that did the trick. And it was Karan Johar who helped Dutt get his mane back.
>
> Realising that it was becoming quite tedious for Dutt to shoot for *Agneepath* bald and then wait till his hair grows out to shoot for *Rascals,* Karan Johar arranged for a celebrity hair artiste to fly down from Nigel Beauty Emporium in North Hollywood to Mumbai and work on a wig for the actor. Incidentally, this is the same place where Hollywood actors including Tom Cruise get their wigs made.
>
> Sanjay Dutt revealed that this was the first time the hair artistes from Hollywood had flown out for an assignment. His personal hair stylist Aalim Hakim is working on the final touches.

His chosen hairstylist Alaim was also the one who gave him his biker sideburns, reminiscent of the ones he sported for *Musafir* and for *Saheb Biwi Aur Gangster 3*. This new hairstyle was the talk of the town. When he stepped out of jail, he had a very peculiar hairstyle indeed and his striking feature was the golden ponytail with his signature Mohawk. 'Inside the jail, my hair used to be snipped by one Mishraji. He gave me this golden pony tail,' he said to the media, turning around to give camerapersons a good glimpse of his new hairdo.

There is an interesting anecdote about Sunil Dutt's reaction when Sanjay started wearing his hair long. He appeared at the dining table one day, sporting his new hair do, and Dutt sahab joked that given that he was finding it difficult to convince producers to sign him up, the new hairdo would make it easier for them to say 'no'. Shortly afterwards, he turned up with an ear stud. One does not know how Dutt sahab reacted to that, but presumably he had not envisioned an era when all that he thought was unworthy of an actor would be celebrated as the actor's signature style and lapped up by the masses.

In a bizarre outburst during a press conference in 2016, Pooja Bhatt, who has been keen to revisit *Sadak* with Dutt, lashed out against Ranbir Kapoor, who plays Dutt in *Sanju*:

'Tell Ranbir that this is not how it works. You have to live, you have to fall, no one can become Sanjay Dutt like that. The generation today, nobody says anything without a PR person, nobody steps out without a stylist. When Sanju cut his hair in that Mohawk style and wore that ganji, it became a rage. I don't think that just by spending weeks with Sanjay, Ranbir will be able to play him. Maybe he needs a few more knocks.'

While a lot of what she said may seem out of context and unjustified (and proven wrong eventually), she got it spot on about Dutt's DIY image styling. In the film *Aatish*, when he first appeared with his own kind of mullet and wore a vest (or a ganjee) for the first time, it became a rage. Salman Khan eventually mastered the ganjee and the shirtless look, but it was Dutt who actually set off the trend. He has been acknowledged as the original trendsetter as far as bodybuilding is concerned in Bollywood by so many others who came after him—John Abraham, for instance, who in many of his interviews credited Sanjay and Salman for starting this trend of macho lead actors.

Moving on to tattoos: Sanjay Dutt is one of the most tattooed actors in Bollywood. Once again, it is a trend that he started off and it was Aalim who created most of these tattoos. He has several tattoos and they all say something about his life. There is a small tattoo on his nape, which has been created by Vishwas Dorwekar of Hakim's Aalim. It is a four-inch Tibetan 'Om' with his sun sign, Leo and his lucky number, one, below it. This tattoo extends from his hairline to his shoulder blade and is an elaborate, intricate inking over his existing lion tattoo. The Tibetan 'Om' represents the first sound that was responsible for all creation.

He had a tattoo done during the Goa shoot of Ajay Devgn's comedy *All the Best*. In fact, it is said that Dutt had encouraged Ajay to get the Lord Shiva chest tattoo that he is seen sporting in *Singham*.

On his right arm, Sanjay Dutt has two samurai soldier tattoos, one below the other. One soldier is in black-and-white and the other is a colourful one. Both are shown with Japanese flowers showering over them. The soldier tattoos are said to symbolize his lifelong struggle, in which he fought like a samurai, never giving in. This tattoo was again done by Vishwas Dorwekar. He also tattooed the word 'honour' in Japanese on Dutt's arm.

When Saif had Kareena's name tattooed on his arm (done, incidentally, by Dorwekar), Dutt also had his wife Manyata's name tattooed on his left arm on Valentine's Day. The latter was designed by Samir Patange. This was not as Manyata but as Dilnawaz, which was her original name (although they had to drop Sheikh, the surname, as it would have become too long). In memory of his parents, he had their names tattooed on his chest. Interestingly, while his mother Nargis's name is written in Urdu, his father Sunil Dutt's name is written in Devanagari script. According to a source, he wanted to depict their secularism with these tattoos. He also wanted to show that they will always remain close to his heart.

On his tattoo agenda, reportedly, is a reprisal of his existing elaborate lion tattoo, which has faded. The lion tattoo on his forearm reads 'Simba Rules', which is said to represent the child hidden inside the man. He also has an elaborate Lord Shiva tattoo on his left shoulder, with 'Om Namah Shivay' in Sanskrit below it. On his right shoulder, there is a fire-breathing dragon, representing the eastern dragon, a symbol of good luck and compassion. There is also a Shiva Linga inked on his right shoulder blade and a Tibetan shloka on his left shoulder blade.

No discussion on Dutt's sartorial choices and his macho look can be complete without a note on his passion for bikes. Till the time he made bikes look cool, stars were mostly known for their chauffeur-driven vehicles. At the most, a Kapoor would ride a pretty two-wheeler somewhere in their films.

But something about Dutt's personality was tailor-made for the bikes that he rode on and off the screen. He is the owner of a Harley Davidson Fat Boy and also has Ducati Multistrada. He loves fast cars—no surprises there—and one of his prized possessions is a Red Ferrari 599 GTB. He also owns exotics like a Rolls-Royce Ghost, an Audi A8 L W12, an Audi R8, an Audi Q7, a Bentley Continental GT, a Toyota Land Cruiser, a Mercedes M-class, a Lexus LX470, a Porsche SUV and a Ducati.

When he played a small role in Shah Rukh Khan's *Ra.One,* he refused to accept any remuneration for the same. SRK instead decided to gift him a bike he was eyeing—the Multistrada 1200.

✯

What is a rock star without his music? One of the first Bollywood stars to profess his love for blues and rock, Sanjay spent long hours on the internet looking up trivia about his favourite bands, chatting on band and musician forums and listening to the latest releases.

He has been a fan of Pink Floyd, Led Zeppelin, Metallica, AC/DC, and Jeff Beck, besides blues, rock and modern jazz in general. In an interview with Rajeev Masand right after *Lage Raho Munna Bhai,* he said he had been listening to 'A lot of blues, I got into it and it comes from the heart, they have some great bands and great lyrics.' During his trial, he often regaled journalists with his knowledge of musical icons, 'Did you know that when AC/DC's guitarist Angus Young duckwalks all over the stage, he covers some four kilometres by the end of the show?' he once exclaimed in an interview with *Arré*.

When Rajeev Masand ribbed him playfully during his interview, asking him whether his love for air guitar as seen on some TV shows and the famous *Dus* promotional song was part of the macho image he liked to portray, Sanjay sounded genuinely offended.

Sanjay: 'I'm dying to learn and if I have the time I will start learning the guitar for sure.'

Masand: 'Why the guitar? Why does everyone say they want to learn the guitar? Is it the ultimate macho thing?'

Sanjay: 'No, it's not about being macho. For me, I have always wanted to learn it, right from school but I never got a chance to.'

An icon and an iconoclast, a man who never played by the rules, although the rules played him. That's Sanjay Dutt for you.

13

The Making of Deadly Dutt

If Amitabh Bachchan was the Angry Young Man of Bollywood, Sanjay Dutt was Deadly Dutt, a moniker he had earned thanks to the way he led his colourful life both on-screen and off-screen. Part of his 'bad boy' image, the starry halo, the charisma and the legacy, were all fuelled by his screen avatars.

The myth of Sanjay Dutt was practically a creation of the film media of the '80s and '90s—especially *Stardust* magazine. 'Deadly Dutt', an inspired title, caught on, and in several interviews the star admitted to keeping up with the 'bad boy image' because the audiences loved it. Whenever he did photo shoots, he was seen with a cigarette in his mouth. Even though, in his time, he was working alongside stars such as Anil Kapoor, Jackie Shroff and later Ajay Devgn, for a long time, his Prince of Darkness crown was uncontested. In his prime, he was giving the media everything that no other actor would dare to provide—a rollicking ride into his universe of drugs, booze, women, bikes and controversies. He was every film and tabloid journalist's wet dream come true. Film magazines loved to play up his follies, his failings and his vices, and wrote creatively about his conflicted character, his emotional turmoils and his tumultuous relationships. Everyone, from drivers and security guards to neighbours and disgruntled former employees and lovers, were quoted in articles that perpetuated this rockstardom. Glossy pages were the perfect arena for Sanjay Dutt himself to rant against his father or his family to launch a blistering attack on the 'bewafa' (disloyal) film industry.

Film writing was in a different realm at that time. Journalists, especially senior ones, had unhindered access to the sanctum sanctorum of the stars they followed and wrote about. The more powerful ones could launch careers and even destroy them with just a headline, a photo caption or a whisper campaign.

A closer, dispassionate look at the articles being written about the Dutts would give the impression that the powerful film journalists were privy to their darkest secrets, most intimate conversations and precious moments. Information flowed freely. And as in the iconic film *Almost Famous,* it would not be unusual to stumble into a journalist in Sanjay Dutt's room, where he would be indulging in bro-jokes.

In those analog days, when stars did not have well-oiled PR machineries or the weapon of social media to craft their public personas at will, they relied on friendly journalists to further their cause, fight their battles and sometimes reach out to their fans.

They were willing to share their truths, their emotions and their problems, and it was a perfect ecosystem of barter.

For instance, when Sanjay Dutt was arrested for the first time, the family went into a huddle. With his future still uncertain, and the AK-56 scandal looming, the family found themselves standing rather alone and plunged into despair. They waited in vain for someone from the film industry—the same film industry that had once put Nargis and Sunil Dutt on a pedestal—to come, to be with them, to show support. But none of the heavyweights or vocal ones dared to show up—except Feroze Khan, Raj Babbar, Akbar Khan, Yash Johar, Anil Kapoor and Raj 'Daddu' Sippy. The family was practically ostracized. At this critical moment, a senior film journalist from *Stardust* was reportedly present with the family, as they bared their hearts. Kumar Gaurav, who was married to Sanjay Dutt's sister Namrata, expressed his disillusionment and a sense of being betrayed. 'There is no support from the industry and we have realized that', he confessed. 'I am not surprised with their attitude. Out there, people just want to play it safe. Nobody cares for anybody. We have come to terms with the fact that we don't have any friends. And what friendship are we talking about here? People swing when the wind is stronger. Believe me, tomorrow when things are cleared up, they will all come along and say—oh, Sanjay, we were always with you. That's their mentality. But at least now, we won't get fooled. We have come to see through all of them.'

This was not the first time the family felt betrayed. Dutt sahab had once said when *Reshma Aur Shera* flopped, the house, which had been a hub of activity, had turned into a graveyard. 'For years after that, not a single person visited us'—he said, bitterly.

'We were forgotten. Then suddenly *Geeta Mera Naam* was a hit and people started rushing in. Friends and well-wishers were back and I was very happy to see them. Nargis would get very angry because I used to be genuinely glad. She would ask, where were they all these months?

'Like I told her then and I say the same thing now, you cannot hold it against people if they have their attitudes. You must love and accept people for what they are. You must not change the type of person you are because of others. It's sufficient for me that those who are my friends have come and met me and expressed their regret about Sanju,' Sunil Dutt said to *Stardust*.

The series of anguished interviews by various members of the family was meant to draw attention to the fact that Sanjay was presumably being victimized. They believed he was innocent and made a strong case. 'You know, they give the example of Divya Bharti's death and because of Sanjay's episode, most people had forgotten about her. It's only after the magazines put her on the cover that people started talking about her again. At that time, things were not going so well with Richa Sharma's family as well. And the family was confident that people would be able to forget things told about Sanjay Dutt by Richa Sharma's family,' argued Kumar Gaurav to *Stardust*.

Nonetheless, when Sanjay Dutt came out of the first prison term, he tried hard to prove his detractors wrong. Disillusioned perhaps with the same media fraternity, he snapped when asked about his physical and mental health, having survived his first brush with prison term. He also used the same film media platform to send out a message to the film fraternity—to the section of the people who had decided to boycott him till he had been absolved of all his crimes. He was bitter. And that bitterness and cynicism dripped from his words: 'It's really strange, but people who made these claims about my level of sanity, had never come to see me when I was in jail, to know what was happening to me. The truth is I am perfectly sane and my jail experience has made me even more so. I have a wonderful and supportive family that has seen me through the crisis. Yes, I didn't entirely have a grip over my life or situation, but I had to handle it and accept it and I turned tough.'

When asked if he was disillusioned as not many people visited him in jail, he shrugged and said, 'Who did, yaar? No one did. The few who did got to see me very briefly and so I feel that no one has a right to pass judgment on people who claim that I was on the brink of insanity or that I have become a raving raging lunatic. I don't give anybody that right. And one lesson I have learnt in life is that you have to protect yourself, and I am going all out to do that.' Had he become bitter with the entire experience? He replied, 'Not bitter—I would say more aware. I believe in certain people, I believe in Balasaheb Thackeray and his convictions, I believe in my father, in Shatru saab, Dilip saab, Afzal. I haven't really lost faith in people but yes, I have become more cautious in believing people.' (*Stardust*)

After he came out of prison, he started shooting for *Mahaanta*. He seemed to be a transformed man—not as reckless as he used to be. He even confessed that he didn't look as boyish anymore.

He seemed to be grateful to have Rhea Pillai around him all the time, supporting him, giving him courage. He also used the media interviews to drive home the point that he had stepped into jail a nervous, incredulous and anxious man, and stepped out a lionheart. Dutt told the media, 'It (jail) wasn't a stigma for me. You have to have a very strong heart to take it all. It's not an ordinary situation and right through that one and a half year, when I was being shuttled back and forth from jail cell to court, nobody said anything nasty to me. I met all kinds of people and what was great was that they all prayed for me. It's weird, you know. People who don't know you have this belief in you.'

Once more, the legend was resurrected. A star, insanely popular with several scars and scandals to his name, is dragged into a high-profile case, goes to jail and walks out a bigger star than when he walked in.

Over the years, both the audiences and the media may have become less enamoured by the Sanjay Dutt story. A lot had happened to the country between 1992 and 2016, when he was sent back to prison. The economy had opened up. Our perception of terror and communalism became more polarized. Icons were being decimated every day, and new ones were being born. Mobile phones had taken over our lives. And a whole new generation had come into place, which had little or no patience with serial offenders. They were far less forgiving, but far more eager to bring down someone who they believed had no moral or ethical claim to their adulation. Those millennials who were clueless about Sunil and Nargis Dutt's real legacy saw Sanjay as just another privileged star kid with a staggering sense of entitlement and a convict who should not have been treated any differently.

But while fewer people seemed to be interested in the Sanjay Dutt story, everyone was interested in the story of a celebrity's rise and fall and rise and fall again. Even when film writers had less and less to write about Sanjay, and legal and crime reporters began trailing him, the myth was perpetuated. In fact, Holla wrote about how 'Sanjay's rank casualness and exceptional obedience in court was interpreted by observers in two ways: Either he is a genuinely humble man, or the artist in him is putting up an act knowing full well that he will get away easy... Any other celebrity wading through the hostile waters of a grievous criminal trial would know better than to play into the hands of prying journalists, but not Munna Bhai. Sanjay, long past the point of caring, could throw caution to the winds.'

On 21 March 2013, when Sanjay was sent back to jail, both the digital and print media were on overdrive. Media watchers were appalled at the high-pitched, exaggerated coverage, which seemed to be born from a deep-rooted sympathy for the star—making him seem more unequal in the eyes of the law than others.

Reactions from the Hindi film fraternity were captured in detail as stars and filmmakers expressed shock, anger and sympathy, extending unflinching support to the actor and his family when previously almost no one had stood by them. 'Some articles covertly supported Sanjay's extension plea till the time he fulfilled his professional commitments (rumoured to be valued at around ₹80 crore), suggesting that several producers could go bankrupt otherwise. No one put out a story or suggested that these producers were taking a calculated risk, knowing fully well that Sanjay would have to face a verdict sooner or later. That would liken their position to stock market brokers whose risk didn't pay off, and perhaps would not help turn the situation around,' said a blistering article in *The Hoot*. 'Most media coverage veered towards gaining sympathy for the actor, thereby exposing their own bias towards the judgement.'

The media was simply playing to the gallery. The readers and audiences were hungry to lap up every bit of this unprecedented event.

Reporters, camerapersons and photographers chronicled every little detail, like who supported him on this journey—family (wife, sister, brothers-in-law), friends (like Mahesh Bhatt), media (the presence of crowds of journalists) and fans. 'The overwhelming attention given to him by everyone, except perhaps the police, would make readers think this was a man wrongly convicted,' wrote *The Hoot*.

The Hindu was neutral and stuck to facts while reporting Sanjay Dutt's conviction, referring the discussion in the court that included his appeal for a lower sentence citing his work done for several charities in the past. However, the report of his surrender was relatively sympathetic and mentioned Sanjay saying that he suffered a blow in his stomach due to 'over-enthusiastic media personnel', thus highlighting his movie star appeal. The actor's lawyer was quoted in the report saying that the star suffered from high cholesterol and arterial stenosis and had therefore requested, among other items, electronic cigarettes, citing withdrawal symptoms if he was asked to totally refrain from smoking.

Hindustan Times filed a report saying Sanjay Dutt feared for his life (from fundamentalist groups) and wanted to surrender at Yerwada Jail in Pune instead of Mumbai. The piece did not point out what gave rise to such fear in the actor, but proceeded to say that the court refused to hear his plea.

The Times of India discussed a havan and other religious ceremonies conducted by the actor's family as well as reporting a list of friends and colleagues who visited him (as did *Deccan Herald*), showcasing the amount of respect and love he commanded among his peers. There were reports of him spending the first night at the jail feeling 'restless' and 'suffocated'. A report prior to his surrender also quoted how he was unused to the poor conditions that prevailed in the jails and how this had spurred a teetotaller like him to 'take to alcohol to calm his nerves.'

There were only a handful that argued that had the star been treated like any other accused in the same cases, he would not have had the luxury to go back to star in box office hits and resurrect his career.

Shekhar Gupta, in his column for *The Indian Express,* said that although Sanjay Dutt was '... talented, vulnerable, gentle, well-behaved... obedient older brother... good husband and father...,' it was not enough to absolve him of his crime.

'Details of everything from his mood swings, recurrence of alcoholism, teary-eyed episodes while dealing with family, havan and other ceremonies performed at his house, items he would be taking to jail (including a mattress, copies of the Hanuman Chalisa and other religious books, mosquito repellant, pillow, toothbrush, paste and soap, as reported by *The Indian Express*) and what he would do at jail (farming, cooking and baking, as speculated by some, considering he focused on carpentry in his previous jail stint), which jail he would eventually go to (Pune, Nashik, Nagpur or Mumbai) and 'pandemonium' at the gates of the TADA court when he came to surrender—all were covered in regular updates,' observed *The Hoot*.

Aakar Patel, however, had a different view altogether. In his *Mint* article 'Sanjay Dutt knows guns,' he wrote:

> I first saw him when he was 21. *Rocky* had been released recently and was a hit. Dutt was staying at the palace of the nawab of Sachin in Dumas, 10 km from Surat. We were there on a picnic and heard the rumour about Dutt. One of us, Tajwar, was related to the nawab and we ran to the palace. The guard opening the gate confirmed Dutt was inside, saying, '*Shooting ho rahi hai* (shooting is on).'
>
> It was, to our disappointment, the other sort of shooting. Dutt was on a hunting tour with friends and, having done some target practice on the grounds, the young men were packing their rifles into their jeeps as we entered.
>
> Dutt had three licensed firearms: a bolt-action Bruno .270 rifle, a .375 Holland & Holland (H&H) Magnum double-barrel rifle and a 12-gauge shotgun... Since he used the guns for hunting, and didn't just keep them on his walls, Dutt was knowledgeable about calibre, range and effectiveness.
>
> In 1992, he acquired a fourth firearm. This was a handgun,

a 9mm automatic, bought illegally and in cash from Yaqub, a man he knew from Dawood Ibrahim's gang.

So, when Dawood and his partners offered him an AK-56 weeks after the Babri Masjid fell, Dutt was already equipped for self-defence, the reason he says he wanted the gun.

Patel wondered why it was that a star living in a Pali Hill bungalow needed a fifth gun for self-defence, especially against those who hated his Muslim mother. After all, as Patel remarked: '...this is a man who wore the teeka on his forehead, sacred threads on his wrist and went to Siddhivinayak temple.'

Added Patel: 'I think Dutt got the gun because it was a cool thing to have.'

On his part, Sanjay Dutt has given enough fodder to feed his image—a bad boy with a golden heart and eventually a man who was a victim of his own destiny.

He said in an interview (*Stardust*): 'My life is an open book and people know everything about it. I do not fear that anything from my life will create a controversy as all my life has gone in controversies. I want to go across the country and speak to people about my life and share my journey.'

Turning a new leaf inside the jail, he claimed to have come a long way from his wild days. Speaking about how he read the religious texts of various faiths in jail, he said, 'I can sit and talk to any maulana or any priest and make sense. I had a small temple, *samne bathroom tha tab bhi mandir tha* (even though there was a bathroom in front of it, I still had a temple). God is in your heart.'

There are some lines from his iconic films however, which may just return to haunt him from time to time. '*Zindagi jeene ka mazaa tab aata hai... jab maut ki ungliyan thaamkar bhaga jaye* (You truly start enjoying life when you feel the touch of death),' he said in *Aatish*. With that, he dares his bestie to a dangerous game of dashing out of a warehouse seconds before it explodes.

If, for decades, there was an effort to make Sanjay Dutt appear larger than his immense frame, by the relentless focus on his troubled life in recent times, there has been an effort to humanize him. And it comes from the film fraternity.

Ranbir Kapoor, who was immersed in his role as Dutt in *Sanju*, said:

> He hasn't been a hypocrite about it (his life). So it's not a propaganda film trying to portray him as God or something. We are trying to show a very human side of Sanjay Dutt, his perils, his downfall, his will to fight, his time in jail, terrorism charges, his drug phase, how he handled his mother's death two [sic] days before the release of his debut film, his relationship with his father. These were human conflicts in his life. He is such a relevant person even today. He is so much loved even today. He is controversial. But when you have Rajkumar Hirani as the director and Abhijat Joshi as the writer and the character like Sanjay Dutt, you are somewhere cushioned.

As recounted before, Pooja Bhatt had lashed out at Ranbir, opining that the younger actor had not suffered enough to accurately portray Sanjay Dutt. Bhatt was perhaps not the only one to feel this way (that Sanjay Dutt had suffered the most among all his peers) once again perpetuating the legacy of a star-crossed star. A man who is the sum total of his mistakes.

In film after film, it would seem Sanjay was forecasting his life. In *Musafir*, for instance, where he sported a designer undercut and beard, and smoked a cigar, Dutt said: '*Taqdeer teri chhutti pe, Maut tere sir pe; baat aise kar raha hai jaise kismat tere bistar pe hai* (Your destiny is on a holiday, Death is on your head, but you speak as if luck is in your bed.)'

It may be noted that other than Amitabh Bachchan, there is perhaps no other star who has had dialogues that have their own cult following. While fans and followers would always draw parallels and relate his iconic dialogues to real events in his life, Sanjay Dutt has done his bit to keep the camera rolling. In an interview with Simi Garewal, when asked why he thinks his life has been an exceptional story of ups and downs, he paused, smiled and said, 'Perhaps I am the chosen one.'

You can expect the frame to freeze at this point, to the tune of dramatic music, wailing guitars or a plaintive violin—depending on which side of the fence you are on. The thing about Dutt is this—no matter how objective you try to remain, he will compel you to choose a side. There has never been any middle path in his life. Neither has there been any middle path in the coverage of his life.

Epilogue

'From the moment Sanjay Dutt walked onto the set, it was an equation set in stone. He was a tremendous presence: focused, disciplined.... You could see the hunger in his eyes for good cinema and the dedication with which he shot this film. It was also so touching to see the unconditional love people have for him and how, despite all the knocks that life has dealt him, he is all heart. You cannot write off Sanjay Dutt. Ever.'

ADITI RAO HYDARI, SCROLL.IN

Aditi Rao Hydari was Sanjay Dutt's first co-star in his first film after his jail term got over in 2015. And her assessment of Dutt on the set would sum up the mood of the industry, which seemed to have been waiting anxiously for the star to get back to doing what he does best. *Bhoomi* was a curious choice for a comeback film. The story of a father who seeks to avenge his daughter, it was supposed to be a tender—tough exploration of their relationship. The film bombed. It was obvious that Dutt was perhaps not ready for it. Yet. Dutt's last cinematic outing before he went in to serve the last few years of his sentence was *PK*. It was a film where he did not have to do much, but it was an important thread—that of Rajkumar Hirani, who was waiting, camera-ready, and focussed on Dutt as he stepped out of Yerwada Jail forty-two months later. But if Dutt hoped to rebuild his image and cast himself as a doting screen dad with *Bhoomi*, the gamble did not quite pay off.

Some reviewers were generous to Dutt. For instance, Udita Jhunjhunwala wrote in *Firstpost*, 'The big differentiator is that this film has Dutt showing us that his wrinkles have their own stories to tell. While the idea of an eye-for-an-eye and taking the law into one's hands is hard to justify, Dutt's performance is affecting. He's tender, he's tormented and helpless, and when he's vengeful, you feel his pain.'

Others, such as Raja Sen of NDTV, had little patience for the man: 'It probably makes sense for Sanjay Dutt to play a slurring drunkard in *Bhoomi*. It makes it okay for the returning hero to look like he has forgotten his lines. More grizzled than ever, Dutt lurches through *Bhoomi* speaking all his dialogues—from the prayers in an aarti to a declaration of bloody vengeance—in the same dopey monotone.'

Namrata Joshi of *Outlook India* questioned Dutt's choice of comeback vehicle: 'Sanjay Dutt hasn't lost his acting chops yet, rather seems to be maturing well. But why did he have to pick up a film this regressive for a return?'

Dutt was looking at finding a spot for himself. 'I am in no denial about my age. I want to play roles that suit my age like they do in the West. On one side we have Varun Dhawan, Ranveer Singh and Sidharth Malhotra, on the other side we have Shah Rukh, Aamir and Salman Khan who are in a different zone. There is no one in the 50+ mature, tough-guy-zone and that is the space I want to be in,' he said to *Firstpost.*

From the reactions of his fans on his social media pages, it is obvious that there are only two kinds of Sanjay Dutt films that work: Dutt as the goofy goon with a golden heart a la Munna Bhai, and Dutt as the cool gangsta of the Sanjay Gupta films. And Dutt seems to have gotten the message, finally. He quickly put the debacle of Bhoomi behind him and signed up films such as *Sahib Biwi Aur Gangster 3,* in which he revisited his trendsetting undercut of *Musafir,* while talks of a Munna Bhai sequel have been swirling for a long time. He also signed up for *Blockbuster,* a multi starrer comedy. Ashutosh Gowariker has announced *Panipat,* with Dutt and Arjun Kapoor starring in the period drama. Subhash Ghai has announced a sequel to *Khalnayak* and going by the reactions of some of the other filmmakers, Dutt may have more crowd-pleasing sequels to revive his career. But his fans have been clamouring for that one film to silence them all—preferably with Sanjay Gupta.

There has never been a dull moment in Dutt's life. Even when he was in jail, there would be regular updates circulated in the media about his love notes to his wife and letters to his long-lost friends in different parts of the world. While his frequent furloughs always made news, there was always something or the other about him or Manyata that ensured that even when he was out of sight, he was never out of our minds.

This transition is interesting because, till recently, Dutt has never really had his way with the media. His interviews—other than the colourful ones given to film magazines of yore—can be painfully boring. He often slips into monosyllables—in fact, the interview with Rajeev Masand was an example of how difficult it may have been for a veteran journalist to get him to speak. He belongs to the generation that did not believe in hiring a PR manager. And he may have paid a heavy price for it. While he was busy ducking controversies and playing snakes and ladders with the legal system, the world around him had changed. He may have been the founder president of the boys club in Bollywood—the 'patron saint of the macho club' as Gups once said, teaching the boys a thing or three about looking the part. But the younger lot, especially his Mini-Me, Salman Khan, turned out to be way smarter than the original. Perhaps he was the alarm that rang loud and clear in everyone's mind. Salman's team of spin doctors, headed by the likes of celebrity manager Reshma Shetty, ensured that he turned his narrative around right at the climax. Dutt's runaway truck had a clueless star at the wheel. Or maybe he was delusional?

The last few years, however, have seen Dutt make amends for his naivete. As soon as he stepped out of prison, he began what can be termed as a PR-overdrive. In a photo shoot with *HT Brunch* magazine, a clean-shaven Dutt, with a designer undercut, spoke about reconnecting with his kids.

Dutt said in the interview: 'When Manyata was pregnant, I always thought I would be a damn strict dad. But with them, I just can't be that! Although I do spoil them a bit, I make sure that when Manyata is scolding them, I don't become the peace broker. I don't interfere. It is wrong to play good cop/bad cop. But yes, after two-three hours, dad might get them a box of chocolates. It is a great feeling to just see them grow up.... We don't waste time with them. They go to school, then they go for swimming, they have their karate classes. I want Iqra to learn the piano, and Shahraan to play the guitar. The other day, Iqra made some cupcakes for me, can you believe that! Now they have even started to decide what I should wear. They pick my T-shirts when we go shopping. They get me toys also! Yesterday Shahraan was very categorical about what we should wear for the shoot today... I feel really bad that I couldn't spend much time with her (Trishala). But today we share a very strong bond. I am very proud of the person she has become. She is a beautiful young lady and very well brought up. And I am forever grateful to her grandparents for that.'

Interestingly, Dutt's twins were not told about his jail term. In the interview with *HT Brunch*, Manyata explained their decision: 'They are still too young to understand what happened... Shahraan's dad is his hero, his role model, he idolises him. I worry for two things. First, it could be too much of a shock for him; he might not be able to justify what had happened or understand why it happened. Second, he might start thinking whatever his dad did back then was cool. We don't want either to happen. They should know that their father was wrong and he has paid a heavy price for that. Not many people would have the courage to own up to what they had done and face the consequences. I want them to understand how it happened, why it happened, and how Sanju took it in his stride. But they are still too young for all that and we don't want to burden their childhood.'

One wonders how far they have been successful in shielding the smart kids, who are so 'tech savvy' in Dutt's words. Nonetheless, the parents say the kids were used to their father being away for long periods of time and they stage-managed the rest.

Dutt, however, has a slightly different take. 'Honestly, I don't fear that my kids will start hating me after knowing my story,' he said to *Hindustan Times*. 'That's the truth, and they have to know it and live with it. I feel it's better if they hear it from me than [from] somebody else. And, of course, once they know everything, they can learn from that, too.'

Dutt's social media pages show videos of him playing badminton with his kids, and recalling his brief, idyllic childhood with his father. There is also an image of the three gathered around a havan kund at home, praying to Lord Shiva. It is an image loaded with subtexts and not-so-subtle messages to critics. There are videos of hysterical fans lining the streets and spilling over the rooftops of small towns where he has been shooting. To another image that has Iqra, Manyata and Trishala as the 'most important women' in his life, a fan has reminded him of how he must never forget the other two women who saw him through his darkest times—Priya and Namrata. The tone of most of these interactions are warm, familiar—almost as if family members are conversing. And no other actor, perhaps, manages to command this kind of affectionate adulation. A mediocre actor who had his moments in some films;

a brat who clearly has had problems with good and evil, right and wrong; a former junkie and a man who played footsie with underworld dons while walking in and out of relationships: There is very little in the Sanjay Dutt story that would endear him to the masses. But we are also a people who worship hero-giri: machismo with a golden heart. Even as he nears sixty and pushes himself extra hard to stay in the game, he will never find himself in an empty theatre.

Fans keep showering him with compliments. They speak of his 'kind heart'. Of his 'clean soul'. They speak of the hardships he has had to go through. In his rise and fall and attempts to rise again, they perhaps see a bit of themselves. And they see the vulnerability and fragility of a star who turned out to be much more human than most people. Stars are known to have conflicted inner lives. They carry invisible scars and excess baggage. But very few actually speak about it. Dutt, on the other hand, has put every bit of his life out there. Call it artless or maybe canny—but as long as he remains the man who went through hell and came back, he will always have sympathetic ears. This may be why he has now embarked on a path of neo-Gandhigiri, wherein he presents his own case study on each and every platform he can get. He speaks with candour and earnestness about his drugs and his Quixotic way with guns and the underworld. But now that the gates of Yerwada Jail have closed firmly behind him, and the Instagram and Twitter updates are crowded with happy images of his friends and well-wishers such as Amitabh Bachchan, Mahesh Bhatt, senior ministers and loads of family pictures—would he still generate as much curiosity? In recent interviews, Dutt has distanced himself from all attempts at telling his remarkable story. He wants to do it himself. For the next generation, he says.

The question is, would people respond to the good guy avatar of the yesteryear bad boy? Not so long ago, Shah Rukh Khan had said that he wanted only to make and be part of films that his kids would be proud of. And then he toplined *Happy New Year* and *Dilwale*.

Dutt is perhaps trying to strike a balance. Making up for the lost time as a father—he never quite got the time and space with Trishala—and as an actor. He knows he cannot do a *Cheeni Kum* or a *Dear Zindagi*. At his age, with his wrinkles and eye bags, he cannot play Sanjay Gupta's leading man. The best option for him would be to mine his real-life experiences while playing roles that hark back to his heydays.

Despite appearing on a Star World show featuring Madhuri Dixit where he placed his former alleged lover and co-star in the same rung as Madhubala, there has been tremendous speculation about *Kalank*, his film with Karan Johar, where Dixit replaced the late Sridevi. Soon as he stepped out of prison, Manyata was trolled for posting a picture of herself at the Dutt residence next to a lampshade that looked like an AK-47. Every time Trishala comes visiting, there are reports on how the step mother and daughter have been bonding. No one still quite knows if the Dutt sisters have settled all their differences with the brother and his wife. Speculations remain rife over Dutt's continuing rift with Gupta. His biopic was delayed because several stakeholders, including Dutt, apparently had problems with the way his story had been told. And Dutt continues to tour cities, giving motivational quotes about what not to do.

Sanjay Dutt may be keen to give himself a bright new future, but his past is the most interesting chapter in his story.

List of Films Featuring Sanjay Dutt

2019: *Kalank*

2018: *Saheb Biwi Aur Gangster 3*

2017: *Bhoomi*

2014: *PK*

2014: *Ungli*

2013: *Zanjeer*

2013: *Policegiri*

2013: *Hum Hai Raahi CAR Ke*

2013: *Zila Ghaziabad*

2012: *Son of Sardaar*

2012: *Department*

2012: *Agneepath*

2011: *Desi Boyz*

2011: *Ra.One*

2011: *Rascals*

2011: *Chatur Singh Two Star*

2011: *Double Dhamaal*
2011: *Ready*
2010: *Tees Maar Khan*
2010: *Toonpur Ka Superrhero*
2010: *No Problem*
2010: *Knock Out*
2010: *Lamhaa: The Untold Story of Kashmir*
2009: *Aladin*
2009: *All the Best: Fun Begins*
2009: *I Blue*
2009: *I Luck*
2009: *Kal Kissne Dekha*
2008: *EMI: Liya Hai To Chukana Padega*
2008: *Kidnap*
2008: *C Kkompany*
2008: *Mehbooba*
2008: *Woodstock Villa*
2007: *Dus Kahaniyaan*
2007: *Dhamaal*
2007: *Shootout at Lokhandwala*
2007: *Nehlle Pe Dehlla*
2007: *Eklavya: The Royal Guard*
2006: *Sarhad Paar*
2006: *Lage Raho Munna Bhai*
2006: *Anthony Kaun Hai?*
2006: *Tathastu*
2006: *Taxi No. 9 2 11: Nau Do Gyarah*

2006: *Alive*

2006: *Aap Ke Dil Mein* (Short)

2005: *Vaah! Life Ho Toh Aisi!*

2005: *Ek Ajnabee*

2005: *Shaadi No. 1*

2005: *Viruddh... Family Comes First*

2005: *Dus*

2005: *Parineeta*

2005: *Tango Charlie*

2005: *Shabd*

2004: *Musafir*

2004: *Rakht*

2004: *Deewaar: Let's Bring Our Heroes Home*

2004: *Rudraksh*

2004: *Plan*

2003: *Munna Bhai M.B.B.S.*

2003: *LOC: Kargil*

2003: *Ek Aur Ek Gyarah: By Hook or by Crook*

2002: *Kaante*

2002: *Annarth*

2002: *Hathyar: Face to Face with Reality*

2002: *Maine Dil Tujhko Diya*

2002: *Yeh Hai Jalwa*

2002: *Hum Kisi Se Kum Nahin*

2002: *Pitaah*

2001: *Jodi No.1*

2000: *Raju Chacha*

2000: *Kurukshetra*
2000: *Mission Kashmir*
2000: *Jung*
2000: *Chal Mere Bhai*
2000: *Baaghi*
2000: *Khauff*
1999: *Khoobsurat*
1999: *Vaastav: The Reality*
1999: *Haseena Maan Jaayegi*
1999: *Safari*
1999: *Kartoos*
1999: *Daag: The Fire*
1998: *Chandralekha*
1998: *Dushman*
1997: *Sanam*
1997: *Daud: Fun on the Run*
1997: *Mahaanta: The Film*
1996: *Namak*
1996: *Vijeta*
1995: *Jai Vikraanta*
1995: *Andolan*
1994: *Amaanat*
1994: *Aatish: Feel the Fire*
1994: *Insaaf Apne Lahoo Se*
1994: *Zamane Se Kya Darna*
1993: *Jai Devaa*
1993: *Sahibaan*

1993: *Gumrah*
1993: *Khal Nayak*
1993: *Kshatriya*
1992: *Jeena Marna Tere Sang*
1992: *Yalgaar*
1992: *Sarphira*
1992: *Sahebzaade*
1992: *Adharm*
1991: *Fateh*
1991: *Qurbani Rang Layegi*
1991: *Sadak*
1991: *Saajan*
1991: *Do Matwale*
1991: *Khoon Ka Karz*
1991: *Yodha*
1990: *Jeene Do*
1990: *Khatarnaak*
1990: *Thanedaar*
1990: *Tejaa*
1990: *Kroadh*
1990: *Zahreelay*
1989: *Hathyar*
1989: *Hum Bhi Insaan Hain*
1989: *Taaqatwar*
1989: *Kanoon Apna Apna*
1989: *Ilaaka*
1989: *Do Qaidi*

1988: *Jeete Hain Shaan Se*

1988: *Kabzaa*

1988: *Mohabbat Ke Dushman*

1988: *Khatron Ke Khiladi*

1988: *Mardon Wali Baat*

1987: *Inaam Dus Hazaar*

1987: *Naam O Nishan*

1987: *Zameen*

1987: *Imaandaar*

1986: *Jeeva*

1986: *Mera Haque*

1986: *Naam*

1986: *Sone Ka Pinjra* (Video)

1985: *Jaan Ki Baazi*

1985: *Do Dilon Ki Dastaan*

1984: *Mera Faisla*

1984: *Zameen Aasmaan*

1983: *Bekaraar*

1983: *Main Awara Hoon*

1982: *Vidhaata*

1982: *Johny I Love You*

1981: *Rocky*

1971: *Reshma Aur Shera* (child artist)

1964: *Memories* (child silhouette)

Acknowledgements

To make this book authentic and factually correct, I refrained from hearsay anecdotes and the many stories floating around on Dutt which couldn't be verified. I am thankful to Mr Nari Hira and Magna Publishing Company for access to their archives, unseen photographs and many rare interviews of Dutt and his family members dating back to 1970. Thank you, Kamalnath, for your support and for burning the midnight oil to figure out all those important documents.

I am thankful to noted author Hussain S Zaidi and his publisher for the excerpts from *I Am Abu Salem*.

After gathering all the information and images related to the subject, I needed someone who would work as my check point. Someone who would see the story from a neutral point of view. I am grateful to my friend and former colleague, Chandrima Pal, for joining me as the editor and guiding force on this project. Needless to say, without her expertise and editorial skills, this wouldn't have been possible. We argued, we laughed and we reasoned endlessly over the past 365 days to make this book.

I definitely thank my friend and film producer Aritra Das, my wife Sarbani Mukherjee, and my parents for being my guiding force. And this wouldn't have been possible without Dibakar Ghosh from Rupa Publications, who had the necessary courage, faith and belief in this project. I have realized that you need an equally encouraging and gutsy publisher to stand by your vision.

Index